THE
COMMON THREAD

Lessons in Leadership and Awareness for Life and Business

COLONEL JIM M. DONIHEE, OMM, CD

 FriesenPress

One Printers Way
Altona, MB R0G0B0,
Canada

www.friesenpress.com

ISBN
978-1-5255-8992-8 (Hardcover)
978-1-5255-8991-1 (Paperback)
978-1-5255-8993-5 (eBook)

1. Business & Economics, Leadership

Distributed to the trade by The Ingram Book Company

TABLE OF CONTENTS

I dedicate this book, with deep love and gratitude to my loving wife Susan and to my three children, Jennifer, Christopher, and Meaghan. Their love and encouragement have fueled my passion for life – without them, this work would not have been possible.

PREFACE

I never thought that I would find myself being in a place where I might be telling my own story. I grew up in a modest home the youngest of four children. I certainly wasn't a leader by any stretch when I was growing up and cannot say that I came to it by nature. My father had served in Canada's Armed Forces throughout the Second World War and often spoke of how he had tried to enlist to become a pilot at the outset of World War II. If you can imagine the folly of it all, he was in his early 20s, had already graduated from a business College in upper New York State, and was a superb athlete. They told him that he was too old, and, in his disappointment, he decided to walk across the street and join the army.

He, like so many of our veterans, rarely spoke of the experiences that he was subject to while serving overseas. Occasionally, however, he would comment about being on the ground while watching the allied aircraft fly overhead en route to their targets and, subsequently, fly over again while they were homebound. Whether in part it was his dream to become a pilot or my own, I was fascinated with the dream of becoming a pilot. So, upon graduating from high school I enlisted in Canada's Armed Forces with the intention of becoming a pilot. That is where my journey in leadership began.

I attended one of Canada's military colleges and completed an undergraduate degree in business administration. While the degree in terms of academics was solid, the lessons I learned that mattered most and which have prevailed throughout my life, were the lessons in leadership and the values that were inculcated early on. The values taught and lived at the military college, those being: Truth, Duty, and Valour; have served me well throughout my life.

I worked hard while I was at the college, and though I did fine in academics, they were not really my thing. I enjoyed the collegiate sports and the opportunity to experience travel and a great number of challenges that I had never been faced with before. I started learning a lot about myself and my abilities in a quest that was as much about learning the limits of my abilities, as it was in answer to proving my own self-worth. I was extremely fortunate at that stage in my early adult life to be afforded opportunities to lead others. I never pushed to be at the front of the crowd as a leader, it just seemed to happen. I was blessed with a deep sense of caring, as well as a desire to serve and to instill fairness and transparency in how things worked. Somehow that allowed me to motivate, encourage, and align people around a common task to make things happen.

Along the way, I discovered myself. I discovered that through hard work and dedication that dreams come true. I completed my pilot training and was selected to fly single-seat fighter aircraft. I discovered that being part of a truly elite group of pilots called for an exacting culture focused on excellence and teamwork – a culture in which second best wasn't good enough. I also learned that being the best didn't mean that you had to have a monstrous ego. Humility and focus were always of greater value than loudness and bravado. I learned that errors can really sting, and sting quickly whether you're operating at 540 knots (620 mph) just 200 feet above the ground in a CF-104 or conducting air combat maneuvering in a CF-18 at 30,000 feet. Sometimes the errors are fatal, and you need to learn from them and do your utmost to ensure they are never repeated.

I learned that true teamwork demands *carefrontation*, a form of accountability that sets the highest standards that you must meet, or you have no right to expect them of others. Most importantly, I learned that caring deeply about the people you lead, the people that you actually serve and who are in your care, is the real glue that binds an organization together. I also learned the rank on your shoulder or the corporate position you hold affords you the privilege to lead and that leading solely based on that rank or position is the weakest form of leadership.

What I also learned early on and what I continued to refine throughout all the various assignments I had in both military and corporate life, was that excellence in performance and mission accomplishment is really all about people—you cannot do it alone. Self-awareness—"Know Thyself"—as a leader will always be key to building teams and harnessing their potential. Whether it be a team of ten, 100, or 5000 people you need to create a vision, you need to motivate, and you need to align people to get from the start line to the finish line in the safest and best possible way. Each of those people will look to you for the highest possible standard of leadership and you don't get to choose when you're being observed or not. You need to live as and be the example that you want them to emulate throughout your journey together. The responsibility of leadership is absolute integrity, and your word must be impeccable.

Along the way, I learned that building a sustainable, high-performance organization goes beyond leadership. The high-performance organization that you want to build will require simple, yet highly effective fit for purpose processes and practices to foster alignment and performance. Those processes and practices need to act in harmony, as a synchronous system, in order to support the alignment and expectations of performance that are necessary from top to bottom throughout the organization. In too many instances, especially in the corporate sector, I witnessed key elements of these various systems turning friends and colleagues within the same company into competitors rather than collaborators focused on their common success.

Throughout my journey, I was privileged to lead or hold senior executive positions in substantial organizations in the military, the public sector, the private sector, the not-for-profit sector, and small entrepreneurial companies. The wide range of lessons and observations that I offer in the following chapters reflect my journey. I bear some scars and some incredibly fond memories from the people that I worked with, the successes we enjoyed and, on occasion, the failures that we succumbed to. I learned that in times of failure it was most important to first look in the mirror, and in times of success to diminish any role I played while elevating the team. My mission was to create a compelling vision and to create the environment within which success could occur. When that happened well, people's true potential always surfaced, magic happened, and great things followed because it's always about the people – they are the common thread.

The chapters that follow will offer a mix of vignettes, templates, and tools that are intended to help you grow personally and develop a sustainable company that is focused on excellence in execution and on fulfilling a purpose that reaches beyond merely making profits. As we move forward, especially as we step beyond the post-COVID-19 era, our workers, their families, and society at large are changing rapidly and expect returns that reach beyond profits. Throughout these various stories, you'll find tools and principles that will serve you in a scalable manner as you seek to build trust, instill a commitment to excellence, actively create the culture you want, foster teamwork and accountability, and finally develop and inspire leadership throughout your organization.

There is a common thread throughout the book because across the array of my personal experiences I have always discovered a *common thread* in each organization—that it is all about people. Success and performance are always about people coming together and aligning around a common vision, purpose, and goals in teamwork and community. The best technologies and nested spreadsheets may generate efficiencies, but in the end, the performance and returns that you generate will always be delivered by people. How you care about them, how you see them, how you treat them, and how you lead them is what it's all about. There is no greater reward than to have some of those team members bump into you some ten or fifteen years after you've had the privilege of working with and leading them, and they reach out to shake your hand saying, "Boss, it was such a privilege to work together and to achieve great things; I'd do it again in a heartbeat, anywhere, anytime."

I share these stories tools and templates in the hopes of helping you develop and grow your business and even more importantly to grow yourself, to experience similar handshakes in the years ahead.

1

TRUST

"The way to make people trust-worthy is to trust them."
– Ernest Hemingway

Trust is the cornerstone of every relationship, every transaction, and is the epoxy that binds the fabric of a social structure together. How you succeed as a leader, or not, in fostering trust throughout your organization will determine how deeply people become vested in achieving your vision. Simply stated, your ability to create a high-trust environment will determine your success as a leader.

You cannot demand that trust simply shows up across the organization. You can't order it up on Amazon—trust is built and sustained over time through your actions. Perhaps there may be a grace period, that benefit of the doubt period when you first assume the reigns or are hired into an organization. But that period is simply a courtesy, the length of which is very largely dependent on the temperature that's present when you step in. Very quickly thereafter, the scrutiny that will evolve into a collective assessment of your trustworthiness as a leader will set in. The scrutiny is nothing to fear; rather, it's something to welcome because armed with the proper mindset and approach to earning trust, your organization, and ultimately you, will flourish.

Trust has to evolve and flow in every direction. A leader needs to know his team is trustworthy, and the reciprocal is even more true.—An individual or team needs confidence that its leader is trustworthy. So—who goes first? Working hard, constantly, to create trust is key. The nature of communications, the clarity of the vision and values, and especially the shared understanding of acceptable behaviours all play into trust's potential evolution. Having identified a few of the considerations related to trust, always know that the consequences (+/-) of how the outcomes and relationships unfold will always be mapped back to the trust barometer in your organization. As a leader, you don't get to choose when your people are observing you so you can tell them, "Look at me now—trust me now." Your people will watch you every moment so as to form their assessment of your trustworthiness and, as a direct result, they will determine whether to put their backs to your wheel. If your people assess you as being trustworthy and they trust in both the vision and how you are striving to achieve results, it will pay tremendous dividends in engagement and success. It will also attract other capable people who want to join the journey because that's the ride they've been looking for too.

As a fundamental element of your culture within which trust is key, the tone, transparency, and manner in which communications occur is vitally important. As a leader, being present and human is extremely important to creating trust. Check your ego at the door and listen, interact, and exchange openly and transparently. Being the leader rarely means that your voice needs to be louder or that you always need to have the answer. The odds are that you will have the answer, but when you don't, have the courage to say so. Be authentic and honest rather than stepping on or deflecting questions or dialogue. If there's a legitimate reason that you can't answer the question or contribute to the dialogue (confidentiality, security, insider issues, etc.) say so, but don't use that excuse as a crutch either. Open, frank communications will go a long way to deepening trust as you move forward. Remember that trust will be strengthened whenever you can personally be present, open, honest, and transparent, and most certainly will not by deflecting, obfuscating, and avoiding.

Trust: Practically Speaking

As I've travelled my journey in many leadership positions, trust has, somehow, always played out. Perhaps because I naturally stand in the space of a servant-based leader: a space where I recognized that it's about the team, it's about the people. As the leader, my role was to create a compelling vision, create an environment wherein success could occur, and then recognize that people are the common thread that will execute on strategy. Especially as the organization becomes larger and more complex, as a leader, you will increasingly be removed from the coalface and become more dependent on engagement and execution by others to achieve your intended outcomes.

I can't say that I ever consciously set out to create trust. I can say that it certainly evolved because of my focus on the common thread that drives everything—people. In recent times, however, I came across a simple equation that truly clarified the attributes of trust and provided insights on how to create it more intentionally. This simple formula takes an abstract concept—trust—and expresses it in a manner that can serve you in every relationship: individual, organizational, at the industry level, and beyond. The Trust equation is expressed through four key attributes.

$$Trust = \frac{\text{Credibility} + \text{Reliability} + \text{Intimacy}}{\text{Self-Interest}}$$

Credibility: drawn from your technical knowledge, expertise, and your ability (authority) to actually deliver on the essence of the interaction. Do you know or have access to the precise knowledge required to satisfy the interaction? Do you have the authority / power to make it happen?

Reliability: measured by the dependability and consistency of your actions, and your ability and consistency for delivering the outcomes to which you commit. Do you keep your word—can I count on you?

Intimacy: measured by the quality of the relationship, the deep understanding of each other's needs and concerns, and the degree of safety required for powerful conversations. Do you see me, do you hear me, is it safe to speak, —do you care?

Self-Interest: the degree to which the other party believes that you are only in this for yourself. Big egos focused only on what they get from the exchange rapidly erode or destroy trust. Another powerful way to reflect on this element is from the viewpoint of Self-Importance. When you strive to diminish and de-emphasize your own self-importance, you consciously increase the importance of the other elements in the equation and the potential for trust to evolve.

The Proof is in the Pudding

My first Command in Canada's Air Force was 410 Tactical Fighter Operational Training Squadron—the Cougars—based in Cold Lake, Alberta. The Squadron was then and remains the unit responsible for the full spectrum of training CF-18 Fighter Pilots, from entry level to post-graduate level capabilities. The unit had been worked very hard as a result of the tremendous operational pace and essentially was a "stay-at-home" workhorse that never deployed as a unit, as a team. Promotions were few and the pride, fun, and fulfillment from being assigned to the *Cougars* was weak. When I first learned I was selected to assume Command of the Cougars, I was hugely disappointed as my preference had been to command an operational CF-18 squadron. In retrospect, commanding the Cougars was one of the best assignments I ever experienced.

Although not armed with the luxury of knowing the trust equation at the time, unwittingly working its components helped me engage the squadron personnel and completely turn the unit around. Within two years, 410 Squadron was transformed from the place few wanted to go into the go-to place on the base. First and foremost, I committed myself to the success of our mission and, even more importantly, to the squadron personnel's success. From the outset, I worked hard to learn the names of every squadron member (some 350 of them) and, as best I could, their families. In that way, every member of the squadron knew that they mattered. I created a degree of intimacy amongst myself and the entire complement of personnel that was not previously present. We found a way to reinstitute unit deployments to create operational circumstances that called upon people to know and depend on one another more deeply. We revised our Squadron vision, mission, and values. We constantly emphasized our vision—"To Train the Best Fighter Pilots in the World"—to re-instill pride, and we stressed teamwork throughout all of our activities. We worked to achieve our vision by focusing on people, leadership, innovation, and technology. At every opportunity, I made a point of emphasizing that people and leadership were instrumental to the way in which we'd achieve our vision.

In a nutshell, the Squadron Chief Warrant Officer (the chief non-commissioned officer) and I learned the names, heard the concerns, trusted, empowered, and set high expectations. We worked very hard and played equally hard on occasion when the opportunity warranted, and we routinely spent time with the squadron members to know them and to be known by them. I worked the maintenance line by refueling aircraft, changing tires, and loading munitions, all the while training as a CF-18 instructor pilot and managing the other needs of the unit. We forged a team that was welded to the vision, how we would achieve it, and the high expectations of each other that were required. In the space of those two years, we completely revamped the training syllabus. We introduced a new and much needed electronic warfare certification, we ensured capable young technical leaders were trained and promoted, and we increased the production of CF-18 pilots while holding the line on costs and improving quality. These outcomes were not the result of orders as people so often attribute to the military environment. These outcomes resulted from strengthening the bonds of trust, providing leadership, and by unleashing the power of an engaged, highly motivated workforce.

One of the tasks I took on to demonstrate my sincere interest in the unit personnel was that of personally penning each of them a birthday card on their birthday. When it was warranted, on the advice of the Squadron Chief and through personal observation, we gave the individual his or her birthday off as an extra day of vacation to enjoy with their family. It wasn't universal so as not to become an entitlement, but that simple act paid many dividends through engagement and increased contributions. Recently, some twenty years later, I met one of the technicians that I served with on 410 Squadron, and the first thing he remarked on was the longstanding appreciation for the penned notes and birthdays he could enjoy with his family. Simple, consistent acts of intimacy and caring for your team will garner trust and deepen a shared commitment to achieving great things.

In another instance the trust formula served me extremely well when serving as the Chief Operating Officer for the Canadian Energy Pipeline Association. Rather than examining the components of trust on an individual basis, we applied the formula through the lens of an industry as we sought to increase trust levels between the multi-billion-dollar pipeline industry and the citizens of Canada. We were able to use the formula to examine myriad stakeholders' viewpoints outside of the industry as it pertained to matters of operational safety, how landowners were treated, and the relationships that we were building with regional, provincial, and national regulatory agencies and governments. The trust formula proved itself to be scalable and extremely useful as we worked to increase trust levels for an industry that was under siege.

The Impact: Safe, sustainable excellence

"When the trust account is high, communication is
easy, instant, and effective." – Stephen R. Covey

One of the immediate benefits that we enjoy in a high trust environment is the ability to move safely and effectively to a much deeper / truer quality of interaction. In a fighter squadron or any operation where execution and safety of personnel is paramount, going quickly and safely—leaving rank at the door—to the root of learning and execution is the quickest and most effective path to sustainable excellence. Trust helps you get below the water's surface to safely discuss the things that matter most.

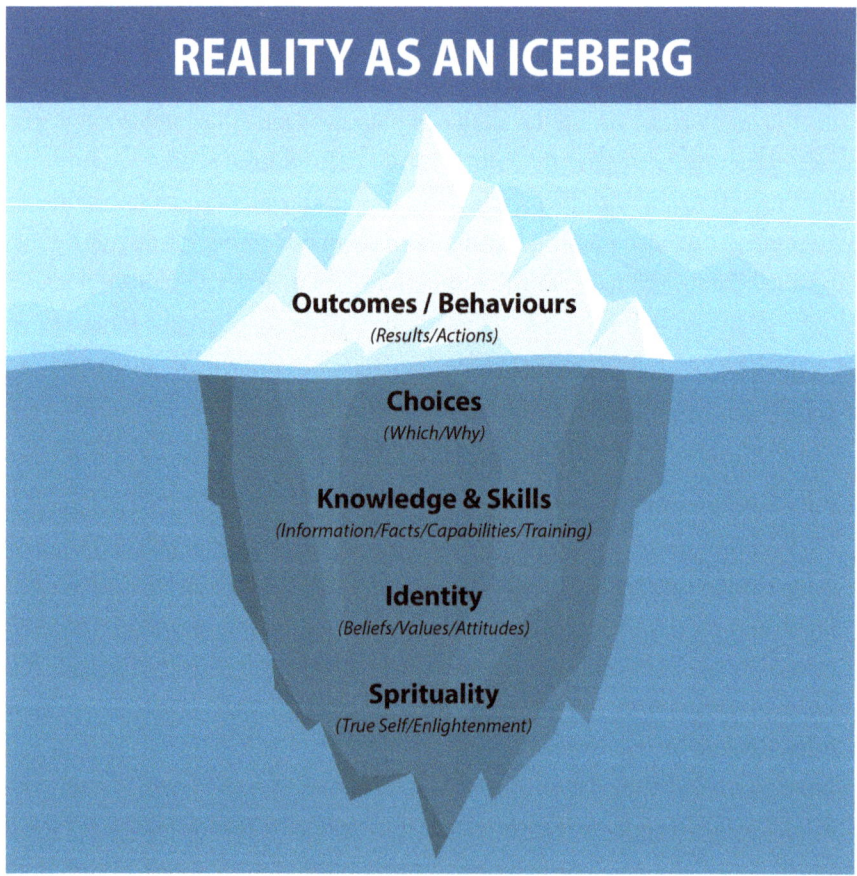

Figure 1 – Reality as an Iceberg

Figure 1 depicting *Reality as an Iceberg* effectively illustrates what is too often the norm in conversations regardless of where they occur. We talk about what happened or the outcomes leading to the way things are while failing to explore what lies below the surface.

To reach and sustain excellence you need to get below the surface—to reach beyond shallow conversations about the weather or weekend plans. We need to explore:

- Choices: which did we consider and why did we select the one we did

- Knowledge & Skills: were they adequate – were there aspects missing or ignored

- Programming: are there beliefs, values or attitudes that unduly influence (+/-) thinking

- Identity: are there underlying elements of ego/identity that influence openness and approach

- Spirituality: what's the degree of awareness of higher purpose and alignment to true self

When we truly succeed in creating a high trust environment, it's safe and expected to get below the surface to explore and clarify vision, the choices that are necessary to achieve it, and the values and capabilities that will be integral to excellence. Importantly, trust provides the permission to dissect operations—without any blame—to identify critical lessons that require action to improve in the next round of execution.

SUMMARY POINTS

- ✓ Trust is the cornerstone of every social structure, every relationship. Your success as a leader will be determined by your ability to build trust in your organization.

- ✓ Trust can't be ordered up—it will be earned, or not, as a result of your actions.

- ✓ Trust is amplified by establishing a clear vision, clear values, and the high expectations that apply to absolutely everyone contributing to sustainable excellence.

- ✓ High trust will lead to high engagement, high productivity, and the attraction of great talent.

- ✓ The trust equation defines the attributes and provides a benchmark for your leadership regarding trust.

- ✓ Trust is personal—look after the well-being of your people and they will excel.

- ✓ Trust creates the potential for the depth and quality of conversations that are necessary for sustainable excellence.

ACTION POINTS

- ✓ Examine the trust formula and reflect on how you transmit on each its elements to your workforce and throughout your life.

- ✓ Examine the Iceberg of Reality and reflect on the depth and quality of your communications: with your workforce, your executive team, and, even more importantly, with your family and friends.

- ✓ Engage your team members with this simple, yet extremely powerful question: "What do we need to do to increase the level of trust in our team?"

2

COMMITMENT TO EXCELLENCE

"Excellence is never an accident. It is always the result of high intention, sincere effort, and intelligent execution."
– Aristotle

I believe there are really only two states in life. You are getting better, you are growing, learning, improving—or you are shrinking, unwinding, or declining. The same is true whether you look at it on a purely personal level or whether you think about it from an organizational viewpoint. So, the invitation then as the organization's leader is to demonstrate and instill a desire—an enduring sustainable desire—to improve for yourself and each individual personally, for your organization to improve continuously. The processes don't need to be complex, but they need to be embedded in your DNA and that of the organization.

To get everyone on the proverbial bus destined for excellence requires that they want to join you on that journey. It requires a safe and inviting environment where people understand a clear vision and mission, focused objectives, and a shared desire to learn and excel while en route to the destination. You need to foster an environment where a team, community, and organization of skilled individuals will come together to share their knowledge, talents, and efforts to achieve valuable outcomes. Undoubtedly there will be mistakes along the way, and the tone you set in dealing with those mistakes as either learning moments or disciplinary moments will dramatically affect people's willingness to climb on your bus and stay on it—or not. So, in the end, clarity of vision and expectations, and a shared focus on constantly getting better in every facet of your operations is what will keep you out of the ditches that line the road to excellence.

I've often spoken with friends about the nature of play in some of the pro sports leagues. Whether it be baseball or hockey, for example, it seems as though there are actually two seasons. In the regular season, regardless of the sport, it seems like they're just hanging out waiting for it to get important. The bats are cooler, the hits are not as hard, and the quality of play just lacks the intensity that's evident in the playoffs—the second season. Most of us don't get to "play in a game" where there are two seasons, especially if you live and work in professions such as the military, first-responders, or in industries where the safety of operations is paramount (either because of the potential for injuries to personnel or the social consequences of accidents). The potential consequences to those people, their families, their reputation, and the environment are unacceptable. Because of that, the need to sustain focus and to excel is of critical importance—the costs are simply too great not to excel.

The challenge we all face is finding the right balance. A pro football team only really executes for sixty minutes per week. They then have a lot of time to study the game films in great detail to identify how they executed and where they can improve. The same is true of the training, practicing, and perfecting of missions that we flew prior to conducting real-time operations in the fighter force. We needed to constantly sustain the highest degree of readiness for our fighter forces to conduct complex flying operations anywhere in the world. The ratio of real-time execution to preparation is minimal, but undoubtedly the stakes are astronomical when it's time to execute—second best in a fighter operation isn't good enough. Though the stakes may not be quite so high, second best throughout the first season means you never get to the second season in pro sports.

In many operating environments, the ratio of operating to preparing is completely reversed with many arguing "I'm constantly in execution—there's no time to get better—I'm too busy doing." That is a false argument that will very quickly put you on a bus to a final destination of decline and failure.

Excellence: Creating the DNA Necessary to Excel, Two Cases in Point

Rankless / Blameless Debriefs

Regardless of where you start your journey with your organization, it's important to get learning practices focused on creating excellence in place. Until it's truly part of the DNA, it's vital that you—as the leader—be present, participate, and set the tone. Exploring how to execute better is never about attributing blame. The exploration is very much about examining where and how the mission's goals were achieved—to capture, celebrate, and share the wins and to identify and work the areas where improvement is necessary. Ground rules must ensure that there's no rank in the room, no positional authority when completing the operational review. In the early days, as leader especially, lean in—fess up and speak to areas where you can and need to do better. Your ability to be vulnerable and speak to areas where you might have done better will create safety in the dialogue vital to the depth and quality of conversations necessary to put gas in the bus on the way to excellence.

While flying as the Wing Commander in Cold Lake, my last flying tour, I made a point of participating in active flying missions to set the tone. Although effectively the CEO of the Wing, I would routinely fly as a wingman in training flights with the operational squadrons. Often there would be a junior two or four plane lead (junior leadership positions) in command of the mission and my role, despite being the senior ranking officer and Wing Commander, was to be the best possible wingman I could be. After the flights during the mission debriefs, in instances where I failed to execute according to plan, I had to own my errors and contribute to the identification of lessons learned in the exact same manner as everyone else. Rank cannot create the privilege of hiding from your mistakes or both trust and integrity will suffer.

In coaching the young leads after the flying missions were complete, I would reinforce the expectations that there were no 'freebies' because I was the CEO. I would reinforce that for them as the leader, regardless of where, what, or who they're leading, that they would routinely get the standard of performance that they were willing to tolerate. If they failed to set and reinforce expectations of excellence, they'd very likely never engender excellence. Equally, our workforces get the quality of leadership that they are willing to tolerate. Employees will either stay on your bus or vote with their feet in search of the quality of leadership they expect. Most notably, your best employees will almost certainly depart your organization if they are not well led or given the chance to develop their full potential. It's important, then, not only to set the bar very high, but to ensure that bar—that high standard of performance, integrity, and accountability—applies to everyone equally across the organization.

After Action Review (AAR) Template

The After Action Review debrief template can be very simple because it's really about instilling a mindset focused on excellence and the discipline required to learn and improve. A simple, yet highly effective debriefing template can look like this:

SIMPLE DEBRIEFING TEMPLATE		
Mission	Clear, specific statement of the mission objectives (outcomes: number, timeliness, quality)	Results (went well / not well) Objectively—how'd we do?
Plan	Based on: Mission, Intelligence, Protocols / Policies, Training and previous instances of execution	Was the plan clear, well-briefed, and understood? How should it be improved for future iterations? Do we employ a standard planning protocol that we constantly seek to improve?
Execution	How did we execute in relation to the plan: Good / Other? • Organizational Factors—resourcing (personnel, equipment) • Leadership—clarity of authorities and accountabilities • Budget—adequacy of funding / spend to plan • Communications—timely, clear, and effective • Partners / Supporting forces—accountabilities, timeliness, quality • Equipment—strengths / deficiencies • Technology—strengths / deficiencies • Protocols / Policies—validity / need to adapt • Training—areas to be reinforced / adapted	Lessons Learned / Action By: • Capture the wins and the learnings through clear statements identifying areas for improvement • Assign accountability to share the wins and fix the shortfalls
Note: There is no rank, there is no blame		

Table 1 – Simple Debrief Template

This initial template for after action reviews will be further discussed during the chapter on accountability.

The Team Knows—Create Community and Ask Them

There is tremendous knowledge and experience resident within your workforce. As a leader, one of your challenges is to find ways to harvest and unleash that knowledge across your operations. In larger organizations especially, there will very likely be multiple operating areas that have significant similarities in their operations. Understanding, then, that highly motivated employees will create solutions to the challenges they face and that those solutions, often worth significant dollars to your organization either through improved safety, reduced consumption of resources, or increased efficiency, are widely applicable to your operations. How do you find and promulgate them? How do you ensure the rapid, effective transfer of knowledge throughout your organization?

A highly effective approach to capturing and sharing the excellence that resides in your organization can be put in place by implementing simple learning forums. While working at a major Oil & Gas company, I introduced knowledge exchange forums that enhanced expertise, identified, and spread improved operating practices, and put the collective wisdom to work on shared problems. One example of such a forum saw us bring together all the lead mechanics from each area operating large diesel engines in support of gas compression and transmission. Before bringing the leads together for a couple of days, we asked them which problems and challenges they were most focused on (technical, maintenance, personnel, supply, innovations) and compiled a concise list of both their challenges and how they had solved them. The information we compiled helped attendees understand that they had often solved issues plaguing some of their peers—and vice versa. The sum of their creativity and solutions were often worth many hundreds of thousands of dollars to the company, and even millions once those solutions could be implemented more widely. The opportunity to live, play, and work together closely as peers over those few days would invariably generate many multiples in value in terms of improvements to operating practices and employee engagement in the months that would follow.

As was the case with the debriefing template, a very simple approach can harness the knowledge that's resident in your organization. An effective template to highlight the expertise of attendees could be:

Individuals Name:	Operating Entity: size / scope:	Contact Details: Phone / Email:
Expertise:	Areas of specific knowledge and operational expertise	
Beg / Burning Issues: (operational / organizational):	Specific operational and organizational issues that are impacting results—how can I fix _____?	
Brag / Biggest Value Add:	Details about operational improvements (fixes, modifications, creative changes) that have added significant, measurable value	
Favourite Website:	Intended to expand learning / knowledge	

Table 2 – Knowledge: Beg/Brag/Borrow

Compiling and reviewing the participants' information provided the organizers and me with deep insights into the common challenges faced across the organization. Discussions amongst participants would also quickly lead to exchanges for the benefit of all on the *brag* front that deepened connections and engagement across the community and delivered tremendous operational value to the company. The bottom line is your people know how to improve operations. You create the circumstances that encourage and unleash their creativity and make it known to peers across the organization.

The Impact: Excellence embedded in your DNA

"Be a yardstick of quality. Some people aren't used to an environment where excellence is expected." – Steve Jobs

Excellence can seem like such a throw-away term. From both a personal level and from the viewpoint of your organization, how truly focused are you on achieving excellence? Clearly there are limits to the time and opportunities you have to commit to continuous improvement and it's necessary to maintain balance between the conduct of operations and focused improvement. The misconception that I've come across too often, however, is that an After Action Review has to be both lengthy and complex in order to be any good. Not so!

When you succeed in embedding a commitment to excellence within your DNA, you will grow, and you will attract people to you who want to achieve great things. They'll climb on your bus, put gas in your tank, and contribute immeasurably to assisting you in reaching your destination.

SUMMARY POINTS

- ✓ Committing to excellence ensures that you will grow both personally and as an organizational leader.

- ✓ Excellence is no accident—it requires a continuous focus on clear objectives, sound execution, and the discipline to objectively review, learn, and improve.

- ✓ Excellence is only achieved in a debriefing environment where you park rank and blame at the door.

- ✓ Excellence means there are no 'freebies' for leaders. Like everyone, you must be held to a very high standard for performance, integrity, and accountability.

- ✓ Your people are extremely resourceful, create opportunities for them to seek and share excellence.

- ✓ It is not a sin to fail—commitment to excellence however means learning and not making the same mistake twice.

- ✓ Excellence is no exception—you will get it, or not, based on what you are willing to tolerate.

ACTION POINTS

✓ Assess how robust and consistent your organization's After Action Review processes are.

✓ Assess how effectively knowledge and innovations are captured and implemented throughout your organization.

✓ Create an opportunity for operational disciplines and technical experts to come together to solve, share, and create community.

3

CULTURE

"An organization's culture is its psychosocial infrastructure."
– Firms of Endearment

The power of culture within an organization is far-reaching. The truth is, whether you're the smallest or largest of entities, you will have a culture. The real question is, "How is it working for you?" Because in the end, it's not charts or spreadsheets or plans that execute to deliver results, it's people. As the key person, the key leader in your organization, the culture you allow to prevail will have a tremendous impact on what you can achieve. Are people really "your greatest asset" or do you treat them largely like any other asset—like a piece of equipment that is to be used, greased, and replaced when it starts to give you a little trouble?

The culture that prevails, like everything else in your organization, will settle and find balance in line with what you're willing to tolerate. If you're not leading with an intention to create a culture that positively aligns with what you want to achieve you will just get what you get. Either way, the culture that results will determine how well your organization functions, who chooses to work within it, and how it is perceived externally. The culture that's prevalent across your company will have a huge impact on your reputation.

It's interesting to contrast how deliberate organizations are in selecting and establishing their corporate brand, the externally facing promises about their offered product and relationships, with how deliberate they are in establishing and strengthening their cultures. Leaders understand the impact of brand whereas they often pay little head to culture believing it's the purview of HR. Culture has the potential to be a powerful *people brand* for you—defining, creating, and sustaining your people brand will make the place hum. People will be attracted and retained or repelled as a result of culture. If you want to attract the good ones and repel the others, then culture shouldn't be left to chance any more than you would leave your brand to chance.

> *"Culture is the domain of leadership—yet it is too often left to HR and never hits the CEO's radar screen."- Jim Donihee*

Culture is a System

Having spent a great deal of my life in the cockpits of high-performance fighter aircraft, I relate to dashboards and systems very well because my life depended on them. For that reason and by no means wanting to oversimplify the dynamics of culture, I became enamoured with the following graphic—Cultural Performance Levers—to depict a few of culture's key influencers. Learning to appreciate them for the dramatic impact they have on your culture, and the interdependency that exists across them all will serve you well. As a system, the levers will greatly affect the performance of your organization because they will have a direct impact on execution, learning, engagement, attraction and retention, reputation, and legacy. To generate some insights, question yourself on:

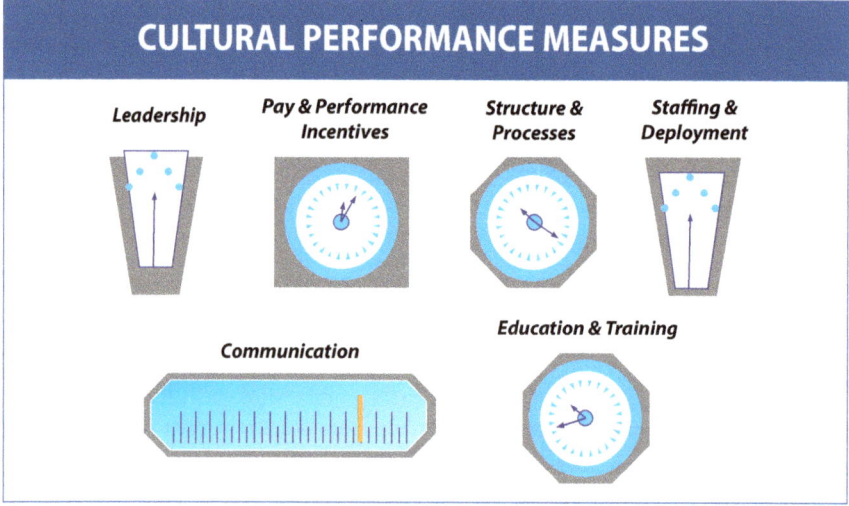

Figure 2 – Cultural Performance Levers

<u>Leadership</u>: How clear and consistent is leadership across the organization, and are leaders held to the highest standard of performance (higher than anyone else who wears the company badge)? Do you train and assess leaders on how they lead, develop, and care about your people, or do you permit your leaders to manage them like any other asset through tables and spreadsheets? Do you personally engage with your leaders, whether selected internally or especially if they're hired or acquired externally due to a merger, to ensure they understand and exhibit the values you want for your company?

<u>Communications</u>: How clear and consistent are communications? Do you actively communicate clear goals, and discuss the meaning of your company values and acceptable behaviours through which they are to be achieved? Do you model open, transparent dialogue and feedback, or do you shoot the messenger and deliver edicts from on high? Do you make time to engage directly with your employees and staff, or are all your communications filtered by those surrounding you?

<u>Education & Training</u>: Do you support continued growth and development across your staff, preparing them for success in the next step in their journey, or do you toss them in—sink or swim—and fire them if they fail?

<u>Staffing & Development</u>: Are staffing processes well established and seen / accepted to be fair and objective by everyone?

<u>Structure & Processes</u>: Are you building a company that is principles- or rules-based? Do structures and processes empower your personnel to innovate, develop, and exercise judgement, or do they push decisions to higher levels than necessary and discourage risk taking? Are learning processes—After Action Reviews—embedded in the organization's DNA to set aside blame and to invite learning, improved execution, and process reviews?

<u>Pay & Performance</u>: Do pay and performance practices reward collaboration aimed at everyone's success, or do they breed competition within and across teams or business units that is detrimental to stakeholders?

If you need greater performance, do you treat them like mercenaries by offering a bigger pot of gold, or do you lead them and motivate them to excel? Are performance metrics related to profits alone, or do they reflect a higher purpose in terms of contributions beyond the spreadsheet?

In the end, the levers will delineate some important parameters that will show up across the organization. The behaviours that are tolerated, or not, will define the real values, norms, and beliefs that will become pervasive across the organization. Your job as the CEO is to make sure the actual agrees with the professed.

Culture: Metaphors, Powerful Windows of Expression

One interesting way to gain deep insight into the culture that prevails in your organization is through the use of metaphors. By posing questions about what it's like to work here that invite the use of metaphors in response, you can unlock a trove of valuable information. For example, in consulting with a small firm at one point, I asked the executive team members and some of their direct reports to complete the following statement:

"The culture of our company is like . . ."

The responses were telling, and here I provide a few examples for you to visualize the state of play that existed, which they needed to grow forward from:

- When the going gets tough, the tough get going—except when conflicts arise, they get swept under the table.

- A jet engine that is still running at maximum take-off power hours after leaving the ground.

- A pristine car that never gets tune-ups to keep it pristine . . . but you can't tell by the paint job or appearance of the body.

- A dysfunctional family with clear and distinctive task wins, but without a soul.

The statements provided valuable insights to the unstated impacts that the pace of work and resulting behaviours were imposing on people. While preserving anonymity and exploring the underlying causes, we were able to dramatically improve the working atmosphere and overall respect and effectiveness of the senior leadership. That increased effectiveness for the executive team then rippled throughout the organization to improve collaboration and operations.

Culture: Defined and Impactful—Guiding a Complex Merger

Shortly after retiring from Canada's Air Force and moving to Calgary, I joined a relatively small Oil & Gas firm—Alberta Energy Company (AEC)—that had a strong reputation as a successful, fast growing entity. After I had been there for a relatively short time, AEC announced that it would be merging with the PanCanadian Energy Corporation to form EnCana, which would result in the formation of one of the largest energy companies in Canada. Many writers characterized the merger as Care Bears (PanCanadian) meets Godzilla (AEC) owing to the stark differences in culture between the two organizations. Recognizing the power of culture, especially when it comes to successfully navigating a complex merger, the CEO led the way to set out and implement the new culture through the creation and release of a *Corporate Constitution*. His intentions were clear in setting out the tenets of the new culture and there was no doubt that it was his domain, his accountability.

In my newly defined role as VP of Organizational Development, I had the fascinating and often very demanding opportunity to serve as the CEO's ghost writer as he set out to create the *Corporate Constitution*. I can absolutely attest that this was not an academic platitude. The CEO owned the Corporate Constitution and wanted it to serve as a beacon for the merged entity, a moral compass that would define the very essence of the new company. The short, vibrant document outlined EnCana's vision, goals, strategy, and how the company would perform; shared principles that every employee would be expected to abide by; employee behaviours that would be valued and those that would not be tolerated; and the expectations of leaders as well as those of team members. Although the CEO held the final pen, everyone was involved both in contributing to and in launching the Corporate Constitution.

The launch of the Corporate Constitution literally involved a handshake, which represented the setting of an accountability contract, between every employee and their supervisor. The act of the handshake represented the shared accountability of both the employee and the leader to uphold the Corporate Constitution. The CEO, while simulcast to the entire international organization, personally shook hands and handed a copy of the document to each of his most senior executives. They, in turn, did the same with their direct reports, and within a few days, every employee in EnCana had received a copy of the document, which bound them to the new way. In a very short time, the cultural levers were all aligned to focus on the future, the new culture. The thing to remember about culture is that it is in balance. Culture is stable and aligned to create the results it's been giving you. If your culture is not generating the results that you want, you need to be very deliberate in how you destabilize and reset it. You can't create a new culture if you're acting in ways that reinforce the 'old' culture that wasn't working for you. You need to closely examine where your cultural levers are set and deliberately reset them to obtain the results you're seeking. Leadership is crucial when striving to change culture.

Culture: Clarity & Alignment—The National Energy Board

Another opportunity to work culture presented itself when I served as the Chief Operating Officer for Canada's federal energy regulatory agency, the National Energy Board (NEB). Needless to say, moving from a highly entrepreneurial commercial operating company to a staid, highly bureaucratic government regulatory entity was interesting. However, the common thread was—and always is—people; people produce results regardless of the nature of the operating entity (private, public or not-for-profit). The other vital, common thread of performance is leadership. The primary cultural levers are the same, perhaps with more or fewer degrees of freedom in movement, regardless of the organization that you are building. So, with people and leadership as the basis upon which to move a challenged, somewhat demoralized organization forward, we took flight. Over the next three years, we assessed, redefined, and implemented the elements of the chart set out below.

Figure 3 – Organizational Performance

People: The Common Thread

En route to being recognized as a Top 100 performing business at the end of that three-year period, we set out a very clear roadmap that ensured:

Strategy: a very clear strategy, integrating both cultural and technical competencies contributing to critical business outcomes, was going to be achieved.

Communications: defined, open, and transparent lines of communication were implemented and, eventually, trust was earned. I often declared that "I can't promise to fix everything that you make me aware of, but if we don't talk, the odds are somewhere near 100% it'll never be fixed."

Consequences (+/-): we redefined performance management, transparently published leaders' goals and objectives to ensure their accountability, and ensured fair, equitable outcomes for all. We promoted some really good people, and we released some really bad apples, which is always difficult in a union environment. This, too, reinforced trust across the organization and ultimately led to the acceptance of introducing performance pay for unionized employees.

<u>Learning Processes</u>: we instituted After Action Reviews and acted promptly to introduce change and eliminate bureaucracy wherever we could to empower the workforce.

<u>Leadership</u>: we placed strong emphasis on developing leaders who could generate trust, delegate appropriately, and who could instill team-work and ownership.

Culture: Its Impact

Tone from the top is vital to culture's creation and sustainment. Culture is the purview of leaders and can't be left to chance if you're truly focused on organizational performance. People deliver results—how they are led, how the organization's pervasive culture empowers them or holds them back will define your company.

I've been privileged to lead in several sectors. In the military, for example, there is no HR and some of the cultural levers such as compensation are not within your control. Many might believe that performance in the military is generated by simply ordering people around, by relying on positional authority. Outside of demanding, high-risk operational environments where room for dialogue may be restricted, reliance on an autocratic form of leadership quickly loses the respect, hearts and minds, and commitment of people anywhere. My time in the Oil & Gas industry often provided examples of extremely competent technical professionals who were rarely trained in how to lead people before being placed in leadership positions. Often lacking leadership experience and cultural competencies, those leaders would generally default to handing challenging employees or relationships over to HR, saying "fix this or bring me a new one" when they were at least equal contributors to the challenges in the relationship. The public service, rooted in bureaucracy and union-based environments, suffers its own challenges. The common threads in every instance are people and leadership.

Properly focused, those threads can create empowering cultures, regardless of circumstances, that deliver excellent results, but you must be intentional.

Like leaders, organizations have personalities that are most often reflective of the top leaders in place at the time. As a result, personalities (and most likely performance) will shift as leaders come and go, but the impact that culture has on organizational performance cannot be overstated. When (1) the CEO doesn't own culture, (2) the tone from the top becomes "do as I say, not as I do," or (3) leaders think they can choose when employees are watching and assessing their behaviours, the culture will quickly become one of survival and cynicism, rather than one of collaboration and contribution with a focus on excellence. With a strong moral compass and compelling desire to lead in the creation of a defined, consistent culture, you and your organization will excel.

SUMMARY POINTS

✓ People produce results—the culture that you tolerate in your organization will define the results you produce.

✓ Your organization has a culture—the critical questions are:

　○ What would your employees say about your culture?

　○ Where is your culture helping / hindering you?

　○ What are you doing about it?

✓ Mergers invite close scrutiny of culture with a focus on what you want it to become—that scrutiny should not be confined to mergers alone.

✓ Your culture is in balance, it's designed to protect itself. If you want something different you have to be extremely insistent on doing it in ways that are focused on the future and diverge from the past.

✓ The Cultural Performance Levers, while not exhaustive, can provide deep insights to how people are influenced to perform.

✓ Culture is the CEO's domain—own it and take accountability for it.

ACTION POINTS

✓ Write out several statements about the culture you want to be pervasive across your company and then examine the Cultural Levers to assess (+/-) how they align in creating your desired culture.

✓ Explore the use of metaphors, through an objective 3rd party, to gain deep insights to the essence of your culture.

✓ Pose this simple instruction to your executive team, your intermediate leaders, and front-line employees: "Tell me where we have breakdowns in our culture and values?"

4

CULTURE: YOU NEED TO MAKE IT REAL

"We can change culture if we change behaviour."
- Dr. Aubrey Daniels

So much has been written about culture that it's very easy to become overwhelmed if you try and soak it all up. As I settled into each new leadership role, the question I asked myself was, "What's the state of play, and how do I move the yardsticks?" There's really no script—no *one size fits all* answer—so you'll need to develop your own assessment and resulting priorities. Remember, always, that culture is a reflection of the leader, and as CEO you are the leader. The HR experts and others are there to advise and to assist in implementation, but you are accountable, you are the owner of company culture.

I firmly believe that success is created by and with people, not through spreadsheets, and for that reason have always taken stock of cultural components as a critical precursor to delivering higher levels of performance. Taking flight in those first months was always most effective when I prioritized getting to "the floor," touring, meeting, speaking with, and listening to people . . . a lot. Set your tone as leader—be who you are because, undoubtedly, that's why you were selected.

As I mentioned previously, the culture in existence when you settle in as a leader is in perfect balance to sustain itself. It is far and away the single greatest contributor to the performance level achieved, especially in relation to the scale of the company. A clear, consistent understanding of the mission across the entire organization is foundational to success. While I served in the military, clarity of mission was ingrained from the earliest days of learning how to plan and execute operations. We learned how to receive and how to give orders in operational environments using simple, yet powerful systems such as *SMEAC* which stands for: Situation, Mission, Execution, Administration (including logistics), and Command (including communications). There was no doubt about the nature and scope of the mission, or the role that every member was to perform as you moved into execution. Nor were there questions about who was in command and who was in support roles.

In moving to the corporate sector in subsequent chapters of my career, I was routinely surprised by how little focus there was on ensuring clarity of mission and accountabilities. In the end, you can have the best technical skills and knowledge available in the market. Still, if you haven't provided clarity about what constitutes mission accomplishment and the various accountabilities to achieve it, execution will waiver. More often than not, there'll be many opinions and lots of blame surrounding the degrees of success that were achieved. By leading with intentionality to make culture real, a culture that's committed to excellence, a culture that you are willing to take pride in, you will create the engagement necessary to stand apart from the competition.

Culture Turnarounds: Two Practical Examples

In the first example, I had joined the National Energy Board (NEB) in late 2004 as the Chief Operating Officer. I was an external hire and replaced a leader who had been elevated to the Board of Regulators. He left behind an organization of about 300 people who were tired and generally thankful that he had moved on. I faced some very interesting challenges as the unionized workforce was generally cynical and burned out. The senior management team was puzzled about why an external hire had been introduced to the most senior leadership position when they, of course, believed there were several viable internal contenders. So, in the context of being the "New Guy" in an unknown and stressed entity, I leaned into my ski boots and took flight.

Over the next several months, I took some very practical steps—with intentionality—to make the renewed culture that I was driving towards real. In every one of my interactions, I spoke from the heart, letting them know the kind of workplace I knew we could create. I told them: "I can't promise to fix everything you make me aware of, but I can virtually guarantee it won't get fixed if I'm not aware of it. And most importantly, I can't do it without you." Note in all of these opportunities where I met with every component of the workforce, I let them know, it's absolutely not about acquiescing or caving to demands. It is very much about understanding the issue, fixing what is warranted and which can be fixed, and explaining honestly and frankly what can't be.

Examples of some practical actions taken to make the culture real:

Coffee Calls: Initially twice a week and subsequently once a week, I held a *coffee call* with randomly selected employees absent from other management. I would provide some personal background and then essentially ask two questions: 1) what's great about working here, and 2) what needs to be improved for you to keep working here? Initially, I received a lot more feedback from the second question, but that changed over time.

We chose the employees at random to ensure I didn't get surrounded by the "keeners" who just wanted to be seen. If there was any bias in selecting employees, it was for those who were more noticeably negative because I knew that if I could gain their trust and acceptance, the turbulence would tend to abate.

Leadership Focus: I met with the extended leadership team and spoke about my personal leadership philosophy and my expectations for them as leaders. We interacted on fundamentals such as vision and mission, the absolute value of people, and the interdependencies and quality of teamwork necessary to excel. We crafted expectations that we would hold each other accountable to, and emphasized not the permission, but the obligation to call each other out on misaligned behaviours. We held a Leaders' Retreat—something that had rarely been done—to build relationships, address communications protocols, and define a vision and the major organizational improvements to be achieved. In effect, we were investing in leadership development to ensure a consistent leadership approach across the organization. Note, I said consistent and not identical; there's a very big difference.

Executive Accountabilities: We posted the entire Executive's Accountability Contracts on our internal website to demonstrate transparency and accountability. The executive and extended leadership team had been pretty good at the "do as I say, not as I do" approach and the transparency and reinforcement of mutual accountability assisted a great deal in reshaping behaviours.

Field Tours: I accompanied field inspectors on facility inspections. I listened and learned, and we came to know each other through the nature and quality of conversations that we engaged in. Invariably they became key voices in implementing changes in expectations, behaviours, and results.

Website / Ask-COO: We initiated an internal website where staff could anonymously ask me any question they wanted about where we were headed. While there's always a risk that the cynics will manipulate the anonymous approach, the ability to deal openly with challenges proved more beneficial than not. When the issue was bigger than an email or web-posting could ever address, I would raise it in our next town hall, or I would meet one-on-one with individuals, so I better understood where / if we needed to make substantive changes.

Performance Management: We reinvigorated individual goal setting, which included behavioural considerations, and performance management across the organization. Most importantly, we emphasized the conversations and outcomes that needed to occur to infuse objectivity and confidence in the organization's performance management practices.

Over the next three years, by implementing these and other initiatives, we reshaped the NEB's culture. We transformed it from a place where cynics abounded to being a high performing people-oriented organization recognized as a Top 100 Employer in the annual ratings surveys. Note I said we, because no matter how big or small the organization—you cannot do it alone. You need to create alignment and engagement to really embed change.

In the second example of reshaping culture, I was hired into Pengrowth Energy Corporation (PGF) to join the executive team as the Chief of Staff. It was an interesting title that very few, including myself, really understood at first. The CEO, who was the owner-founder of the corporation, had the interesting habit of knowing what he needed, hiring the right individual, and just throwing them into the mix, letting things sort themselves out. The interesting observation here is that as a leader, you won't always have clarity around the nature of the role you're moving into. A major element of your task may well be to eliminate confusion, clarify in which areas you can make your greatest contributions, and to then move forward. In this instance, I was accountable for all of the support services, including HR, which came with the requirement to sharpen the culture around commitment to execution.

I found it very interesting to be an operator at heart in a support lead's role. In many ways, it prepared me well to support the CEO as a full member of the executive team and to refocus the culture. PGF presented an interesting opportunity to examine how the commodity-based Oil & Gas company was situated in Western Canada's petroleum industry. The company was structured with several distinct operating and supporting units, which was very common in the industry. The commodity industry's overall mindset has to be around efficiencies and cost control, given that you're effectively a price-taker for your product. Knowing that reality, it was informative to assess how effectively teams performed; how they understood their interdependencies, how they learned and exchanged information, and how consistently leadership was practiced across the organization. Once I got my feet on the ground, I convinced my colleagues on the leadership team of the merits of taking stock of the baseline on leadership and culture.

We designed and conducted a simple survey of the entire extended leadership group of approximately sixty people from across the company's 800 employees. The survey results accurately portrayed the reality of a company that had grown rapidly through the acquisition of diverse assets and the people who came along with them, without placing any intentionality on the company culture that was to prevail. In short, the PGF leaders had tolerated the culture that unfolded and had not worked with intentionality to make it real.

To provide some insights into the survey results, you'll find a select few of the key and very telling responses in the table below. You'll then find brief details of some of the initiatives that were implemented to "make it real."

Example survey questions and results were:

EXTENDED LEADERSHIP TEAM—"STATE OF PLAY" SURVEY		
Question	**% Agree / Strongly Agree**	**% Disagree / Strongly Disagree**
We have a clear and well-articulated business strategy.	59 %	41%
We measure progress and hold each other accountable.	60%	40%
We stretch to achieve break-through performance.	35%	65%
We work as one team regardless of location, department, or functional group.	44%	56%
We document, share, and apply lessons learned to improve.	54%	46%
We strive to develop new leaders for succession and renewal.	42%	58%
<u>Note:</u> the entire, simple yet effective, 25 question survey yielded deep insights		

Table 3 – Sample "State of Play" Survey

Analysis of the survey led to some very candid conversations, which reflected on the evolution of the company's culture and provided compelling reasons to make it different, to make it real. It was a company that had grown rapidly, focusing on the acquisition of assets, the associated spreadsheets, and those tied to them. Few if any efforts had been expended to create a team, strengthen alignment, or improve operations' consistency. In a commodity-based industry that was experiencing considerable upside, that approach was both predictable and survivable. However, to evolve into an operating entity that would stand the test of time and be able to achieve and sustain excellence, it was clear that a focus on culture and making it real was required. The target was not a feel-good organization, but one that was highly responsive, operated effectively, was highly accountable, and shared knowledge with high expectations of everyone who wore the company logo.

The conversations awakened an understanding of the critical need to engage employees as full business partners in creating an environment that more broadly contributed to success, an environment that was worth sticking around in to make a contribution. The conversations also awakened the employees' ability to help determine how the future would unfold.

Direct and frank feedback presented to the extended leadership team, and then to the entire workforce declared the following:

Figure 4 – Cultural Evolution

The survey results formed the baseline in identifying cultural gaps that needed to be addressed with intention to advance towards creating an organization that would stand the test of time. It was time for a concerted effort to "work on the business and not in the business."

Highlights of a few key initiatives that were implemented include:

Leadership Development: We introduced a program focused on leadership development to reinforce values, understanding of strategy, the ability to engage in constructive two-way straight-talk, and teamwork.

<u>Rewards & Compensation Redesign</u>: Rewards and compensation mechanisms were reviewed and completely redesigned to promote excellence, while also emphasizing teamwork and collaboration, especially across the executive team.

<u>Learning Protocols</u>: Simple lookback protocols were developed and implemented with a strong emphasis on improvement and not focusing on blame.

<u>Employee Communications & Town Halls</u>: Sharing the survey's themes through employee communications and town halls created an understanding of where the company was headed and a very positive buzz for the future. Demonstrating progress in a few key areas affirmed commitment and reduced cynicism.

<u>Board of Directors</u>: The survey results and, more importantly, the resulting action plans were shared with the Board of Directors to demonstrate transparency and to lock in on action plans.

As the various cultural initiatives took root, employees quickly moved to a place of greater pride and engagement. Once we introduced a focus and enhanced employees' ability to contribute, greater attraction and retention, greater employee satisfaction, and improved operating results followed.

The Impact: Make it Real, make it a culture you've established, not one you simply tolerate.

So much has been written about culture and the power it wields in affecting organizational results. In all of my experiences, I can say it is absolutely true. When people know that you care about them, that you are working to ensure they make a meaningful contribution that's aligned with their purpose, and that of the company's, they will go all out for you. They can tell immediately when you view them like any other asset that needs a little maintenance and is to be replaced if it makes too much noise. On the other hand, they know immediately when you come from a place of servant leadership. When you come from a place of fair, caring, and authentic leadership and work to establish an embedded and consistent culture, they will still come up to you years later proud of having been part of your team, proud of having given you their all, because they know you gave it yours.

SUMMARY POINTS

✓ Success is created by and with people who partner with you, not through spreadsheets. Work for them as you hope they will work for you—all out.

✓ To set the culture and make it real, you need to invest yourself and not hand it off—you need to work "on the business and not in the business."

✓ Vulnerability is not weakness; it demonstrates humanity and engages. Be yourself, lead with humility, and let them come to know you—be real and not contrived.

✓ No matter how big or small the organization is, you cannot make it real alone. Enlist your leaders to identify the gaps and craft high expectations of one another—then make it happen.

✓ Lead with intentionality to create the culture you want, not the one you'll tolerate; otherwise, you're no more than a passenger on a bus, driven by someone else, that'll never get up to speed.

ACTION POINTS

✓ Take stock of where you are —you personally and your company and determine if it's too comfortable.

✓ Put this simple instruction to employees you come in contact with: "Tell me how we can improve the culture and performance of our company."

5

TEAMWORK

"No one can whistle a symphony.
It takes a whole orchestra to play it."
– H.E. Luccock

Teamwork doesn't just happen. Assuming that teamwork will just work is going to see you leading or playing as a member of some very dysfunctional teams. For that reason, you need to learn early on how to create and lead successful high-performance teams.

Interesting, too, is the reality that the teams resident within your organization are like microcosms of the organization as a whole. Build highly successful teams, knit them together, and create the conditions for them to succeed more broadly, and your organization will be on the right track. As you start to think about teams and teamwork, I want you to think about these three questions:

1. Why is it that you're open to the need to practice and perfect key skills fundamental to winning when you're playing in a team sporting context?

2. In that same team sporting context, why is it so important to learn and practice the plays, the roles, and the system overall?

3. Why are we so amenable to the coach's critical role in a team sporting context, whereas we are far less inclined to engage a coach to enhance our team performance in business?

The answers are straightforward—you need good fundamental skills as a basis for higher and more complex levels of play. Understanding the various roles, plays, and the system is essential to winning execution. Finally, a skilled objective coach committed to the team's success adds immeasurably to the team's growth and success. Very few, very few player-coaches succeed in high stakes professional settings.

A desire to improve, combined with focused practice, increases the team's ability to anticipate the play, improves the flow of execution, provides a depth of knowledge and interoperability across players to deal with injuries and contingencies, and significantly improves your chances of winning. Too easy, you say, I get it. So, the question that's important to think about is if we "get it" and understand the need for that approach to improving team play in sports, why is it so absent from our workplaces? Why are there so many dysfunctional teams in the workplace, and why do we put up with it? Why do we so often throw a bunch of experts into a room and assume they will succeed?

I love the quote chosen to introduce this discussion on teamwork. As you learn and grow in experience as a leader, the metaphor of the symphony is very powerful. The evolution that you'll travel from learning how to read music at the outset to a destination where you're conducting a symphony, where every instrument ebbs and flows in perfect harmony and synchronicity should be emblematic of how your company operates. You can't just throw a bunch of musicians on a stage and expect perfect flow and harmony to happen. They may play the music, but it'll never approach the depth and synchronicity that a well-practiced orchestra would deliver.

The same is true of your teams, whether it be your executive team or any of the operating teams that you lead. A bunch of professionals thrown together may get the job done, but the chaos and confusion experienced will lead to conflict, errors, delays, costs, and challenges that will have a tremendous impact on their ability to create success. It's particularly essential that you create a solid high performing executive team because that team, more than any other, will be scrutinized for the way it operates and how it sets the tone for the entire organization. That team, in particular, has to make sweet music. In short, people wouldn't buy tickets to that unpracticed orchestra performance, and neither should you expect shareholders to invest in an organization where teams are in disharmony.

Practical Example: Teamwork

"Remember teamwork begins by building Trust. And the only way to do that is to overcome our need for invulnerability." – Patrick Lencioni

I had been consulting with CEOs and senior executive teams for several years when I was invited to begin some work with the executive team of a mid-sized energy company that was growing rapidly. The CEO, and the entire team, for that matter, were brilliant technically. Many of them had worked together before when they had built and sold a previous company. It was a fine example of highly-skilled, high-performing individuals who had come together to build something great, but this venture was bigger and more complex and was taking longer to unfold than the previous iteration. This iteration required growth, not so much technically, but from the standpoint of '*team-ship*' and leadership skills. Over the space of about fourteen months, they dove in and evolved to a very different place, a much higher level of team-based performance.

It takes real courage and openness for you, as a leader, to scratch beneath the veneer of your team's workings, but the gains for your business and you personally will deliver very strong value. This team's journey serves as an excellent example you can draw on to strengthen your team. This is the *Reader's Digest* version of the steps we took.

Start by taking stock of the team, from both your point of view and, more importantly, from theirs. The crucial first step is to commit; dedicate quality time as a team to get better. This is often not a comfortable space for people, especially in the highly technical disciplines, because you will be working towards new degrees of openness and vulnerability that some will characterize as being similar to having a root canal done.

We dedicated one full day together per quarter, as well as dedicating some one-to-one time between sessions between myself and the members of the executive team. Without being pedantic, there's huge value in speaking to some models to invite discussion that will lead to the "how's that working (or not) for us?" questions. We started by reviewing the attributes of great business teams and then conducted a team assessment based on the work by Patrick Lencioni—*The Five Dysfunctions of Teams*—to take stock.

The team assessment provided some very telling observations that led to some of the most powerful conversations the team had never had. For a set of very high-performing executives, the survey results, while not a surprise, set the hook for their desire to improve. Highlights, or perhaps I should say low-lights, of the survey that compelled conversations to improve were:

TEAM DEVELOPMENT SCALE SAMPLE QUESTIONS / RESULTS	
Question	Score (1 – 5 with 5 being high)
1 To what extent are the most difficult issues put on the table? [never/always]	2.5
2 How are differences or conflicts handled on the team? [ineffectively/effectively]	2.8
3 To what extent do people give and get feedback on the team? [never/always]	2.9
4 To what extent do team members know and care about one another's personal lives? [don't know/care – know/care deeply]	3.0
5 The extent to which team members are passionate and unguarded in their expressions? [closed/masked – open/unguarded]	3.1
Note: Adapted from Patrick Lencioni – Overcoming The Five Dysfunctions of Teams	

Table 4 – Sample Team Development Scale

They knew the results were telling. Without tabling the most difficult issues for example, it's hard to imagine how an executive team can be effective. The risks associated with failing to address difficult issues in a high-stakes, capital intensive industry are formidable. Leaving them unaddressed or accepting sub-optimal solutions could be catastrophic for safety of operations and the future of the company.

The results of the survey were reviewed over the course of several hours and the observations led to several valuable follow-up actions. Examining the attributes of great business teams depicted in figure 5 , in conjunction with the results of the team assessment survey immediately set that team on a new and more positive trajectory.

Figure 5 – Attributes of Great Business Teams

You will need to consider a number of factors that impact the overall effectiveness of your team. Factors such as "age & stage" related to the maturity of your team, not in terms of the individuals or how long it has been in operation, but in terms of the maturity indicators it presents. Whether individuals have been members of the team throughout, there are a number of new team members, or even if reporting relationships have changed will impact the effectiveness of the team. For this executive team, over the previous twelve months there had been extensive change, both by way of growth in numbers and in reporting relationships for some of the team members. It was a very good example of having created an assembly of experts without having focused on nurturing the team, and as a result its effectiveness had digressed in some ways. To add some focus to the principle of community, we started every meeting with a check-in that invited dialogue beyond business and started conversations about personal health and experiences. Strengthening community and affinity created permission for meaningful relations and authentic conversations about how the team was working, which in many instances were more valuable than conversations about the work the team was doing.

Working with your team, as a member of that team, to focus on team fundamentals—working on the team rather than in the team—will deepen understanding and lead to powerful conversations that will dramatically improve your effectiveness. The following figure outlines some really valuable considerations they reflected on.

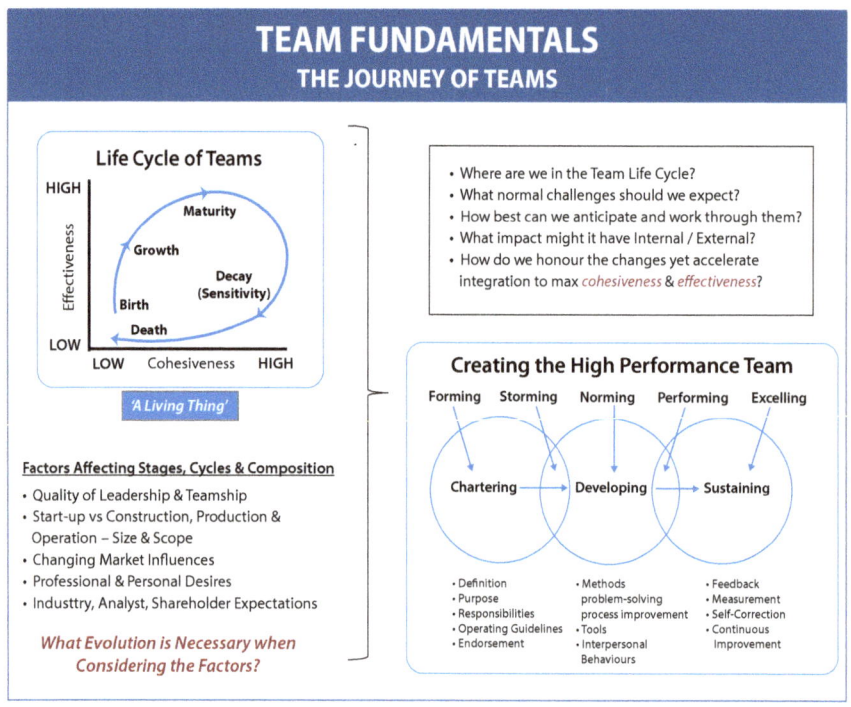

Figure 6 – Team Fundamentals & Considerations

<u>Life Cycle of Teams</u>: Teams are living things that ebb and flow as members come and go and as purpose evolves. Teams may be created, altered, or disbanded. Knowledge of the interplay between effectiveness and cohesiveness will permit you to lead the team and grow it to maximum effectiveness in the shortest timeframe possible.

<u>Creating the High-Performance Team</u>: Being deliberate about working on the team to accelerate the evolution between the Forming and Excelling stages, especially considering how to sustain the team as members come and go, will pay huge dividends. The team assessment will provide a very insightful snapshot of the health of each of the characteristics needed at each stage.

As leader, it's critical for you to create and deepen the invitation to undertake honest dialogue, otherwise you will create cynicism and frustration about the value of the experience. You, as the principal leader, as the CEO, need to show the way. In this instance, the team found it very useful to establish some operating principles that they all agreed to endorse and to hold one another accountable to. Behaviours change as a result of knowledge, maturing beliefs, and constructive feedback—they all signed onto and did their best to put into practice the following principles, which can serve as a strong example for any executive team.

EXECUTIVE TEAM – PRINCIPLES OF CONDUCT

- *I will build TRUST* - *by delivering results, by engaging in respectful challenge, by listening, and by considering and encouraging alternate views.*

- *I will foster open COMMUNICATION* – *by asking questions and actively participating in the discussions, & ensuring open dialogue.*

- *I will seek and provide CLARITY* - *in my communications with others, ensuring understanding exists through proactive questioning & meaningful reporting.*

- *I will RESPECT the chain of command* - *if urgency requires it, I will ensure I close the circle with leaders and respond to the request.*

- *I will Commit to the Executive team* *to shape, respect and support the decisions made in the team, by taking accountability to deliver my part in the agreements.*

Figure 7 – Sample Executive Team Principles of Conduct

In the months that followed, demonstrating their collective commitment to improve, they worked on nudging each other to stay the course and generated considerable improvement in their interactions. The principles not only created permission, but they also created an expectation for frank focused dialogue about the work they performed and how the team worked. The principles also introduced some meaningful banter that strengthened cohesiveness and increased the team's overall effectiveness.

Teams that excel possess strong competencies both in completing the task roles—that is, the "doing" of the work—and exhibiting key competencies in fulfilling the relationship roles critical to supporting one another and creating community.

The example of this team working *on* the team as well as performing the work *of* the team offers you a powerful lesson. They had the courage to take stock and assess where they stood, and they dedicated the time and considerable effort required to grow together. Their transformation relied on: coming to know one another more deeply, unleashing the power of vulnerability, and on their shared commitment to excellence.

SUMMARY POINTS

- ✓ Teamwork doesn't just happen—you need to work on the team to accelerate its journey to excellence and winning execution.

- ✓ Mastering the creation of high-performance teams will provide competitive advantage.

- ✓ Your executive team, in particular, must be exceptional.

- ✓ Demonstrate the courage to take stock by objectively assessing your team's development and how it measures up against the attributes of Great Business Teams.

- ✓ Understanding team fundamentals will provide deep insights into the journey you're on.

- ✓ Team operating principles will clarify teamwork and hold everyone to account—including you.

- ✓ To excel, teams need to master both task- and relationship-related competencies.

ACTION POINTS

✓ Assess your team's quality of play (team development)—what are you tolerating and leaving on the table due to gaps in team play?

✓ Review your team's Principles of Conduct for currency and effectiveness—if you don't have any, engage them and build some.

✓ Meet with each of your team members and ask them to candidly respond to: "Tell me how we can improve the effectiveness of our team." Prioritize and act on their responses.

6

LEADERSHIP

"Before you are a leader, success is all about
growing yourself. When you become a leader,
success is all about growing others."
– Jack Welch

Leadership flows from the top—it's your personal brand and the indelible mark that you will leave on everything you do. As it flows throughout the organization you're creating, leadership will be a marker that creates a polarity: it will either attract or repel. As you build, especially at the outset of growing your business, it's exclusively your brand and approach that will set the tone and expectations. As you continue to grow and you become increasingly reliant on others to lead, both internally and externally, the practice of leadership cannot be taken for granted and should never be set aside or handed off. Leadership is your accountability—it's that plain, it's that simple.

Leadership will be the common thread that galvanizes and engages people around your vision. The polarity, the charges that emanate around leadership in your company, will either attract or repel people. The descriptors—great, mediocre, or weak—that precede the calibre of leadership prevalent in your company will be key in setting the charge (+/-). Great people will be attracted to great leadership because they know they'll be empowered and held accountable to succeed, while, at the same time, growing and learning. On the other hand, great people will be repulsed by weak leadership due to the presence of blame or the absence of vision, clarity, achievement, or trust.

For that reason, you will need to learn and develop throughout your journey, so it will be extremely important to look in the mirror and assess objectively how your leadership is developing and adapting to the changing needs of your company. The view that "Leadership and learning are indispensable to each other," coined by John F. Kennedy, will especially hold true for you as your company evolves. There are too many companies that have stalled or failed because the owner-founder was unable to grow and adapt to the changing demands they had to face. Deep technical competence may be key during your company's initial growth stages. In contrast, leadership and soft skills will become vitally important as you grow and add more people and layers of complexity. By failing to grow and adapt, irrespective of your grandest desires for the company, you will become the choke point that stalls its growth and continued development.

To avoid that all too common pitfall of stalled growth, surround yourself with trusted advisors and coaches, and lean into your humility, recognizing that you won't have all the answers. The ground you are covering has been covered before, and there are many excellent resources available for you to draw upon. Whether it be coaching, consultants, or CEO syndicates where CEOs come together to serve each other as advisory boards, reach out because you will learn more rapidly and accelerate your performance by leveraging the knowledge, networks, and experience of other leaders. Whether it be a coach, an advisory board, or a formal governance board, remember that very few great teams emerge without a coach, and the role of player-coach is extremely difficult to play.

Engage your courage, embrace your humility, and say to them: "Tell me how I can most improve as a leader."

The following table, adapted from Jack Welch's work, can help you set out your personal vision and the work you need to do in order to grow as a leader, and to sustain the level of excellence required to build a great company. There are no shortcuts, and you can't attain the next level of solutions by remaining fixed in your current level of thinking.

PERSONAL LEADERSHIP - JOURNEY TO EXCELLENCE	
Ambition	Create stretch goals and plans to meet them—embed accountability mechanisms to push you forward
Vision	Where will you and your company be, personally and professionally, in 3, 5, and 10 years
Confidence	Grow your abilities and knowledge to underpin your confidence—scrutinize and identify your own abilities that must stretch to grow
Risks	Establish the facts, calculate the odds, decide, and act—prioritize the areas you'll most need at the next level of performance
Commitment	Commit proactively and engage both mentally and physically—you must be 100% committed, anything less is slow drip poison
Excel	Measure yourself and your company, strive to excel at whatever you do
Circumspect	Strive hard, admit mistakes, learn constantly, and improve relentlessly
Lead	Step forward—live the example that others want to follow and be aligned with, reduce your self-importance, and encourage others to grow and excel
You are the creator, not the victim, of everything that is going on! **Adopt a 3rd party perspective to observe your personal** **and your company's (+/-) performance** **How do you and your most trusted advisors assess yourself across this spectrum?** **How will you close any gaps? How will you leverage your strengths?**	

Table 5 – Personal Leadership Considerations

In addition to your personal growth, give thought to how you want leaders in your company to be trained. They will look to you for the style and accomplishments that are required to be part of your leadership team. Spend time with them and engage with them in conversations that clarify the boundaries that will prepare them for leadership roles in your company. Don't make them guess.

There are essentially two options available to train your leaders: in-house or farmed out. Regardless of which you choose, it's critical that you continue to support them on their journey beyond the training. There must be some clear expectations surrounding technical, business, and people skills they need to acquire to succeed in leadership positions. Ongoing support will ensure the training is more than a discreet intervention, an anointment, and a launch into the deep end to sink or swim. The price of failure is too high and often results in departures. Either the new leader isn't ready, and they're subsequently dismissed because they flounder, or the talent they're to lead becomes disenchanted with the poor calibre of leadership and leaves. Either way, there's considerable pain and turmoil which can be easily avoided with proper development and oversight. The cost of turnover is an intangible that's difficult to find in the financials, but it will induce tremendous impact on risk and operations.

Practical Example: A Cohort of Leaders

The group looked at me, bursting with enthusiasm, already looking forward to the next time we were planning to get together in a couple of weeks. The presentations and discussions that we had just completed with this cohort of leaders made them come alive with interest in reading, discussing, and improving their personal leadership skills. As a result of the time the CEO had dedicated with them a few weeks ago, they knew what he expected of them as leaders in this rapidly growing company, and they had just finished a lively debate about what it all meant. Supported by HR and, more importantly, by several of the operational VPs, they were finding their voices, stepping up to challenge each other, and own their individual behaviours and leadership styles. They were coming to clearly understand that consistency of leadership didn't mean they had to be clones of one another; rather, they had to embrace the company's principles and apply them according to their personal style in consideration of the people they were leading and where they were working in the company.

This cohort of leaders had largely self-selected from amongst the *best and brightest* when we put out the call to all those interested in forming a Community of Practice (CoP) of leaders interested in learning and growing at Pengrowth. The group was comprised of managers and directors from across the company and a variety of professional disciplines. They were already busy people, but they were hungry for opportunities to grow and participate more broadly in where the company was heading, so they made time, as committed leaders always do. It was obvious they were coming together as more than a group of individual leaders; they were becoming a strong team of leaders. They had already come a long way since the CoP was formed several months ago, and there was little doubt, they were more engaged and making a difference in how results would be delivered. Furthermore, as they came to understand that the company was keen to invest in developing them as future leaders, their loyalty and belief in the company's future deepened by the day. They had a better understanding of their shared reality, their support for one another was growing, and the ability to reach out, challenge, and contribute meant they were not alone when faced with difficult leadership situations. They were learning—and proving to themselves—that in leveraging and supporting one another, they were delivering better and more timely results. By being in service to one another, they were achieving more.

Looking back over the past several months, getting to this place where the momentum was now established to grow forward, the recipe I had executed in my capacity as Chief of Staff had been straight forward:

- <u>CEO Leadership Vision</u>: I'd worked with the CEO to help him clarify his personal vision surrounding leadership, beyond technical and financial matters, as well as his ability to speak to it.

- <u>Leadership Team—Clarity</u>: We worked to establish a shared view on leadership principles, created alignment on how they would be enacted by the leadership team, and how we'd hold each other accountable to model the outcomes.

- <u>Cohort of Leaders</u>: We identified the high-potential leaders and initiated the CoP focused on leadership to strengthen knowledge, consistency, and alignment across the organization. To complement the leaders' external training courses, we created the CoP of Leaders to establish context and consistency appropriate to Pengrowth. We met for two hours bi-weekly with occasional half-day meetings when we had external speakers. The CoP adopted a results-based model that embedded:

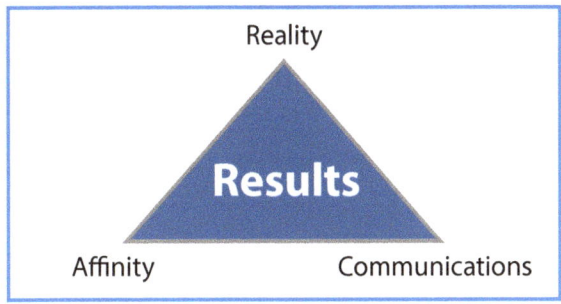

Figure 8 - ARC Triangle

- Reality: We developed a clear and shared view of the reality they were experiencing. Reaching consensus on critical topics such as accountability, culture, quality, priorities, and values helped define the way ahead and significantly improved consistency across the company. They achieved a shared understanding of the challenges they each faced in meeting their individual accountabilities, as well as how the interdependencies crossed structural lines. Armed with a deeper understanding of their shared reality and how they contributed collectively to the company's success, they learned that by being "in service" to one another rather than being in competition, they would achieve far more.

- Affinity: By spending time and having some fun together, the sense of community was strengthened, and barriers dissolved. As the barriers dissolved, they were able to identify priorities and focus on improvement targets they all owned.

- Communications: Truth telling improved markedly as perceived agendas were set aside and trust within the group improved. They felt more empowered, engaged in healthy challenge, and communicated more openly to accelerate results.

Leadership Equals Results

When you consider the journey that you want to travel, the vision that you want to achieve, understand that your leadership will be the marker that needs to enlist and align the efforts of others. As you succeed and your company grows, so too will the complexity and criticality of the decisions you'll need to make. You won't have all of the answers, so it will be important to develop a network of trusted advisors who care enough about you to hold you accountable to grow and to live up to the vision that you establish. If they really care about you, they'll practice 'carefrontation', meaning they won't just blow smoke at you and tell you how wonderful it all is; they will leave you no place to hide along your journey to success. That quality of feedback will be instrumental to your continued growth and development—do not shut it down. Retain your humility because if your ego precedes you into the room, it will deny you the invaluable gift that candid feedback offers.

Decide how you want to develop leaders in your company and ensure they have regular touchpoints with you to experience how you embody the commitment to achieve great things. Inspire them with your energy and passion, empower them to challenge and ask difficult questions—hold them accountable to challenge because they will need to own and infuse your vision into their operating areas and teams. Ensure that you train your leaders to hold true to the principles that you want to be reflected across your company, so there is harmony and consistency of approach, not simply carbon copies. Speak to the ethos of leadership across all fronts: technical, business, and especially in relation to people and community. Because in every endeavour, it will be people who will deliver the results. Lead and foster an environment founded on vision, clear roles and accountabilities, and a relentless desire to improve.

SUMMARY POINTS

✓ Get clear on your perspectives surrounding leadership, especially in relation to your own strengths and areas requiring development.

✓ You will not have all the answers—be circumspect and surround yourself with select, trusted advisors and coaches who will practice carefrontation and hold you accountable.

✓ Develop your leaders—don't leave it to chance; the price of failure is too high. Spend time with them, engage them, empower them, and listen to them to remove barriers and remain relevant.

ACTION POINTS

✓ Invest in your own development—constantly raising your own competencies and consciousness will prepare you for the next round of challenges (through foresight rather than hindsight).

✓ Engage your leaders to ensure understanding and consistency of approach.

✓ Identify and invest in your leaders—they are your future.

7

ALIGNMENT

'Building a visionary company requires
1% vision and 99% alignment.'
– Jim Collins

Alignment, like leadership, flows from your office as CEO. It must begin with a laser-like focus and clarity of your vision and what you are going to achieve. Ensuring, then, that everyone who works for your company gets on and stays on the same page as you is your accountability. Imagine a large complex telescope that so clearly magnifies and presents the image of a distant star to you. In a nutshell, that's the definition of alignment. The complex glass optics, perhaps many layers deep, are perfectly shaped and polished and held in exactly the right position by the housing in order to focus the light from that distant star. Without the perfect alignment of those various components, each playing their part to perfection, there's no light to collect and focus, no image to present. Absent that precise alignment, the results you seek cannot be achieved.

Alignment in your company and the potential that it presents to assist you in achieving great things, like the telescope, is no different. In fact, it's critical.

Most importantly, you need to know what you're aiming at because that defines the path. Articulating the vision and leading the creation of strategy to achieve that vision is one of your key accountabilities. Ensuring that the vision and strategy are fully understood by everyone in the company is paramount. You will need to make sure that the various elements of your company are properly designed, they are in the right place at the right time, and they are in the hands of skilled operators who are engaged and passionate about achieving your vision if you want to excel. When you first start your journey, it's pretty simple to achieve alignment if you only have a few employees. Everyone knows each other. It's easy for them all to sense your passion and to understand where they fit in the puzzle. Everyone can see clearly how the puzzle will be incomplete if any one of the parts is missing or fails to do its job. As you grow in numbers and complexity, it becomes increasingly difficult to ensure everyone shares the same passion and understanding for your vision or how it's to be achieved. Your job, your leaders' job as you grow, is to ensure that there's a deep and consistent understanding of vision, strategy, goals, roles, and processes required to get there—to achieve results together.

> *"Building alignment is the logical next stage after crafting a vision.*
> *Building alignment is the act of gaining buy-in for your vision and it's*
> *absolutely critical in moving from imagination to reality."—Davis*

In the same way that teamwork thrives on a smaller scale because roles are clear because everyone knows where they fit into the scheme of what the team is to achieve, the company needs to be aligned and thrive on a larger scale. Alignment provides that critical common thread that provides every single person with a clear sense of purpose and meaning in terms of their unique contribution to achieving the vision and results that the company sets out to accomplish. The commonality of purpose and commitment creates an efficiency that accelerates everything by permitting goals to be achieved without constantly hitting obstacles around execution. It sets people up to act selflessly rather than selfishly to achieve the company's required goals and outcomes.

To achieve alignment, you need to make sure that the strategy—the What—as it cascades throughout the company is supported directly by the culture—the Who / How—in order to achieve results. The 'How' is set out through the culture that will prevail throughout your company. The values that you reinforce will define how business is conducted, and ensuring they are understood and adhered to is equally important to understanding and execution of strategy.

In the end, it's people that will deliver the results, so strong alignment in terms of strategy and culture will ensure that they are collaborating and completing one another, rather than competing with one another and negatively impacting results. Strong alignment improves trust because people can be empowered to do the right thing, in the right direction, confident in their contributions, and aware of the interdependencies and roles that they each play in delivering excellent results.

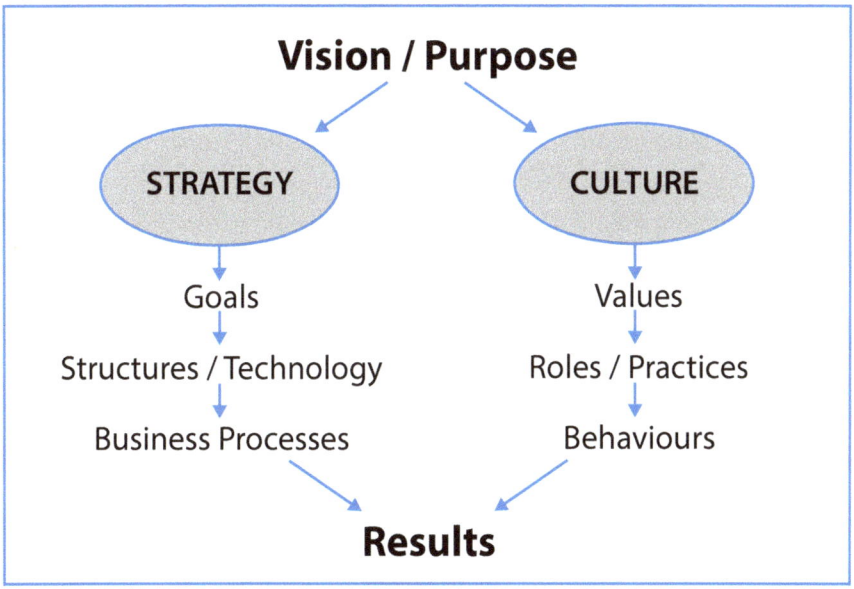

Figure 9 – Alignment of Strategy and Culture

Alignment in Military Operations

Alignment is critical to mission accomplishment and, for that reason, military operations rarely experience vagueness in relation to vision, purpose, and the roles everyone is to execute. There are friendly forces and there are enemy forces and the purpose is clear—neutralize the enemy forces. From the beginning of our military careers, we learn to give and receive orders, which clearly articulate: 1) the mission / goals to be achieved; 2) the supporting forces and technological platforms that'll be employed; and 3) the command structure detailing clear accountabilities that each formation is to achieve. While there are always healthy rivalries between the various combat elements, there's an abiding respect for the capabilities that each component contributes to achieving the mission, and those rivalries are absolutely set aside when operations commence. The interdependencies, related to execution, between the various friendly elements are known and the culture has been shaped around selfless teamwork and sustained excellence from day one.

Fighter Operations—Selfless or Selfish

The typical fighter squadron is comprised of about 300 people, of which only about 25 are pilots. While the pilots may be the people who fly the jets and deliver the final result, that could never happen without the expert efforts of the other 275 service men and women. Like any small company, there's all the usual administrative functions to be staffed and carried out. However, the largest component of personnel assigned to the squadron is devoted to maintaining the aircraft and their complex systems, and to arming the aircraft with the appropriate weaponry needed to complete assigned missions. Only once the jet is loaded and flight worthy can the pilot go airborne.

Fighter pilots are an elite group, highly trained, competitive, and often endowed with egos that match or even outstrip their skills. Like any team or organization, when the egos begin to overstep reality, collide with one another, and undermine mutual respect across the various teams, people will find a way to let you know.

Working as the Commanding Officer of 410 Operational Training Squadron, we had the role of training all of Canada's CF-18 Hornet pilots. The instructor cadre that I worked with were some of the most experienced Hornet pilots in the world, certainly the most experienced from within the Canadian cadre. The student pilots were generally new pilots that were learning not only how to fly the CF-18, but how leadership and teamwork were so vital in a fighter squadron. Occasionally, one of these new gents would overachieve in relation to ego – ego trip, and the support crews always found a way to get the message across.

One case in particular saw a second tour pilot training on the CF-18 repeatedly treating the ground-servicing personnel with little respect for the important work they performed. When it came to a boiling point, he ended up in my office complaining about the fact that he hadn't succeeded in getting airborne on any of his last six missions. Just prior to taxiing for take-off, the ground crew always perform a "last chance" check to visually ensure everything is fine with the aircraft and it's safe to fly. In each of his last six missions, this gent was ordered to shut his aircraft down because the ground crew observed something, they deemed to be unsafe. Actually, they were delivering the message that "we're a team, and while you may fly the jet, no matter how big your ego is, you won't get it off the ground without us." The discussion we had in my office focused on leadership, humility, appreciation, and alignment. His singular actions and egotistical attitude were very misaligned with our culture, which emphasized teamwork to generate outstanding results. I directed him to spend time looking in the mirror and "invited" him to recognize that he goes nowhere without the dedicated support of the 275 service personnel. Hoisting the lessons aboard, he lowered his importance, aligned himself with how we generated outstanding results, and went on to become a superb leader and a very capable Hornet pilot.

Alignment: Every Person Trusted and Empowered to Do the "Right Thing"

One of the roles I fulfilled while working at EnCana, a multi-billion-dollar Oil & Gas firm, was facilitating three-day leadership development workshops for mid- to strategic-level leaders in the company. The workshops were focused around the professional disciplines, and in each instance involved around thirty-five attendees from across North America. The forums provided an excellent opportunity for those leaders to come together, get to know one another, learn of their successes, and conduct Masterminds on challenges they all faced. The forums also provided the CEO and Executive Team members the chance to present on the strategies and objectives in play to create outstanding shareholder returns. During those three days, the attendees were afforded an excellent window into the CEO's and his most senior executives' plans, and, equally importantly, attendees were afforded the opportunity to constructively challenge and learn from the executives.

The most important person in terms of creating successful forum after successful forum was the administrative professional that I worked with. Simply put, she was outstanding. She took exceptional pride in ensuring that every detail related to the conduct of the forums was looked after. The details were many and often fluid, and knowing they were expertly managed permitted me to focus on the content delivery and facilitation of the strategic discussions. She wasn't looking to be on the stage; she excelled and took great pride in knowing her contributions were indispensable to the forums' successful conduct. She was completely aligned with the aim of the forums, fully trusted to excel, and, often, go beyond expectations. The quality of her work positioned the leaders to stand up and talk about pride and excellence across the operations of the company because we were living and benefiting from details that were flawlessly executed. In her own selfless expert way, this administrative professional demonstrated the power of alignment by consistently contributing to the success of our leadership forums.

Alignment—Its Impact

Whether it's individuals, teams, or business units, you need to determine if they're out of alignment and work swiftly to correct it when they are. Assessing alignment and constantly working to strengthen it is the work of leadership, and routinely involves employee surveys. Making sure that everyone knows the company's vision and key strategic elements, and how they map to their team and individual objectives will set everyone up to contribute to success.

"You've got to think about the big things while you're doing the small things, so that the small things go in the right direction."
– Alvin Toffler

When you take the additional step of including considerations related to your customers and how they are either served or impacted by the way your company executes, you can draw on another vital consideration related to the results you deliver en route to achieving your vision. There are many sophisticated tools available to assess the key elements surrounding alignment, and the following example provides insights into assessments you should objectively conduct.

SIMPLE ALIGNMENT DIAGNOSTIC		
Discipline / Questions	**Score 0 - 10** 0 - Strongly Disagree 10 - Strongly Agree	**Total**
Strategy		
Organizational Strategies are clearly communicated to me	7	
Organizational Strategies guide the identification of knowledge and skills I require	6	
People are willing to change when new organizational strategies require it	5	25
Senior leaders agree with and model the organizational strategy	7	
Customers		
There's a prioritized list of what customers care about for each of our offerings	5	
We're provided with useful information about customer complaints	4	
Strategies are periodically reviewed to ensure we meet critical customer needs	5	17
Processes are regularly reviewed to ensure they contribute to customer satisfaction	3	
People		
Our organization collects information from employees about how well things work	2	
My work unit / team is rewarded for our performance as a team	8	
Groups across the organization collaborate to raise customer satisfaction	5	15
When processes change, the impact on employee satisfaction is measured	0	
Processes		
Leaders care about how work gets done as well as results	5	
We review work processes regularly to assess how well they are functioning	6	
When something goes wrong, we correct the root causes to learn and avoid it in the future	6	19
Processes are reviewed to ensure they contribute to strategic goals	2	
Adapted from Organizational Dynamics Inc. (Lobovitz 1997)		

Table 6 – Sample Alignment Diagnostic

The scores are illustrative to provide input to the visual diagnostic to show how the employee responses paint the picture of alignment. Even a simple survey such as this can provide valuable insights to important dimensions that are critical to high-performing, results-based execution. The resulting alignment snapshot, understanding that the perfect score would be 40, provides powerful visual impact highlighting areas providing an invitation for improvement.

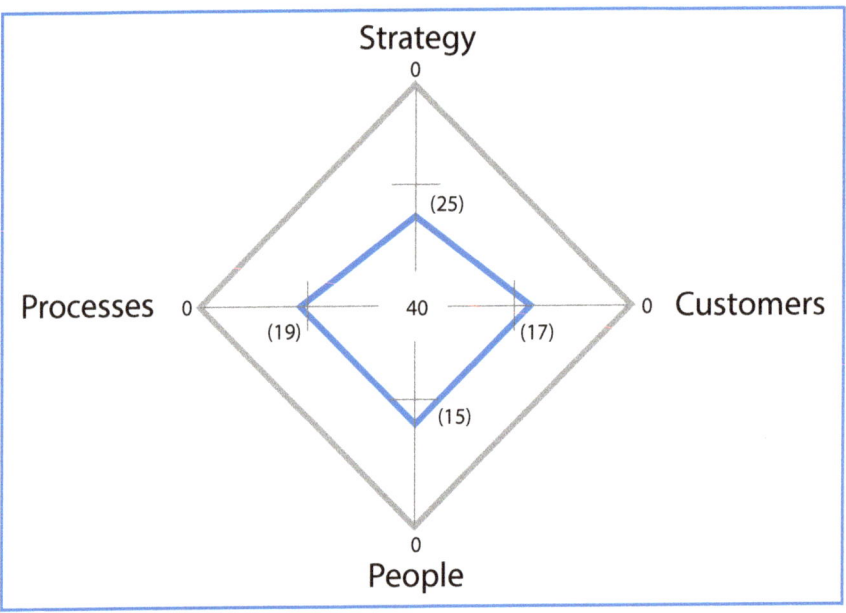

Figure 10 – Alignment Snapshot (Lobovitz 1997)

SUMMARY POINTS

To effectively transform your vision into reality, your company needs to mirror the telescope made up of complex components that are constructed and operated in perfect alignment. You need to point that telescope at the vision you want to achieve and then infuse your people with the passion, desire, and collective sense of direction, contribution, and meaning that will empower them to do the right things the right way. Encourage them to achieve even more as you praise them for success. Encouragement is proactive and will align them to the path.

Effective alignment demands that the What—the strategy—be supported and aligned with the Who / How. Do not lose sight of the fact that people deliver results. You will always get what you are willing to tolerate and that goes for both the What you get and the How you get it. Lead them, align them, empower them, and watch the magic happen.

✓ Alignment is the accountability of leadership, which begins with the CEO and depends on a crystal-clear vision.

✓ Alignment is critical to effectively transform your vision from imagination into reality.

✓ Alignment is the common thread that provides line of sight for every person through the strategy to achieve the company vision.

✓ Assess alignment; don't take it for granted and work aggressively to correct misalignment—it creates confusion and wastes resources.

✓ Alignment is challenged by scale, especially during times of merger—ensure you escalate your work on alignment as you grow—it will pay great dividends.

ACTION POINTS

✓ Assess and embed alignment practices, especially as you grow.

✓ Engage your employees as you move about the company to ensure your workforce is aligned around strategy and culture.

✓ Act swiftly to correct the course of areas found to be out of alignment.

8

SUCCESSION

" The true measure of sustainability for a leader in
building a business is forethought to succession."
—*Jim Donihee*

If you really want to build a sustainable organization whose life will extend long beyond your time at the helm as a CEO, you need to think about depth of personnel and succession. Thinking about succession from the outset will help you with scalability and risk management throughout your company's challenging growth stages. As the CEO, it is your accountability to ensure that any critical failure points are identified and either eliminated or mitigated. One of the best ways to deal with these challenges right from the time you first open your front doors is to be thinking about succession, not only for the most senior people but for everyone that plays a key role either by virtue of function or the critical knowledge they possess.

Adopting a succession mindset early on is going to help you create a solid foundation for your company that is based on the vision, values, and behaviours that you define as being critical to your success. Important to know as well, is that thinking about succession and planning for the future is a leadership function and not the sole purview of HR. Undoubtedly HR will provide valuable assistance, but ensuring the future of the organization is a leadership accountability.

During the early days, depth across various roles is a luxury that you may not be able to afford. For that reason, you may have no choice but to go to the street to hire the talent required for you to succeed. Hire carefully because, in addition to importing skills and knowledge, you are importing attitudes in leadership styles and the execution of processes that may or may not be a strong fit for your developing culture.

As you grow in size and scale, however, the transition towards developing your own leaders who are well versed in your vision and organizational culture is an objective that will hold great merit for you. My experience in the military, like that of an elite sports team, always kept the "next man up" philosophy in consideration. In combat operations, just like on the sports field where losses or injuries occur, the game doesn't stop when someone goes down. Ensuring that you have leaders and skilled knowledge workers ready to step forward is key to ensuring the immediate continuity of your operations and long-term sustainability of your growing company. The way you set up growth, development, and succession is going to say a great deal to your employees about whether they should become truly vested in your company. If you routinely hire senior managers and executive leaders from outside the organization, the best and brightest who are coming up from within will see no future for their advancement and will look for opportunities outside the organization. However, if you're able to invest in and grow your future leaders from within your organization, you will earn their loyalty and their commitment to making your venture a success.

The basis for selecting your leaders has to bear scrutiny. For that reason, a performance management system that provides credible, consistent, objective data needs to grow into place. You will know your system works well when people are nodding and shaking the hands of those who are promoted, rather than mumbling amongst themselves wondering how the heck that happened. Furthermore, the performance management system that you adopt needs to ensure future leaders are being identified early, and that the competencies they need to develop, as well as the experience they need to gain, form part of their regular coaching discussions. In this way your performance management system will perform the very important role not only of identifying replacements for people who depart, but more importantly for developing the future leaders your company requires.

Planning for the Future

One of the best examples of considering succession requirements was the organization I lived within the first twenty-eight years of my working life. The Canadian Air Force has a very well-defined performance management system that identifies leaders from the ground up. It is based on a suite of competencies—technical and leadership—that have been defined for every one of the positions. Coaching and development are a key part of the process, and results are reviewed at least annually. Based on the reviews that every unit in the Air Force performs, personnel are broken into one of three categories:

- A Level Individual (Best 10-20%): This category represents people demonstrating an extraordinarily strong performance track record who are also deemed to have a strong potential to perform very well at least two levels higher than their current position. They are moved more rapidly, placed in challenging positions to further their experience, and monitored closely to ensure they continue to learn and grow. This cadre of people will also be provided with additional opportunities for professional training to develop the competencies that are required to lead at more strategic levels.

- B Level Individual (Core Performers 60-80%): This group of individuals represent the "salt of the earth" performers who are at the core of your business. They provide very strong contributions to the successes you will enjoy, but they're individuals who will progress at a rate which is more closely aligned with the average, perhaps due to differing levels of commitment and competency from those identified in the first category. This type of individual performs well and takes pride in the contributions they make, but they don't demonstrate the desire and drive to reach the highest levels in the organization.

- C Level Individual (Underperformers 5-15%): These individuals represent your weakest performers. For this category of personnel, it's necessary to identify corrective measures, which may include coaching and training, to move them up into the B category; reassignment if they're not in a position that is best suited to their abilities; or, in the worst case, the development of an exit strategy for them.

The following three charts provide a simplified view of the outcome of performance conversations that occurred twice per year. The organization chart provides a powerful visual representation of the conversations, and the final chart, once completed, provides good insight to the depth of talent that resides in the organization. The reports stemming from the talent conversations that took place constantly rolled up to the higher levels so that we gained an in-depth view of the bench strength that existed across the entire Air Force. When it came time to consider promotions, selection panels were formed comprising several individuals from the same profession, as well as an honest broker from a different profession. The honest broker served to question and eliminate any personal biases that could arise when selection panel members knew individuals under consideration for promotion. All of the members of the selection panel were at least two ranks higher than the openings being considered in order to have the experience and strong perspective of the leadership and capabilities required at that next level.

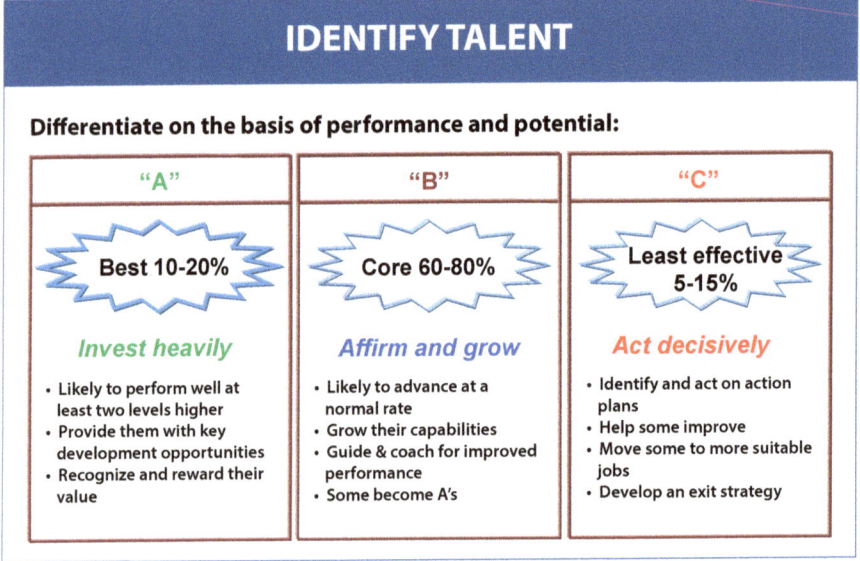

Figure 11 – Talent Categories

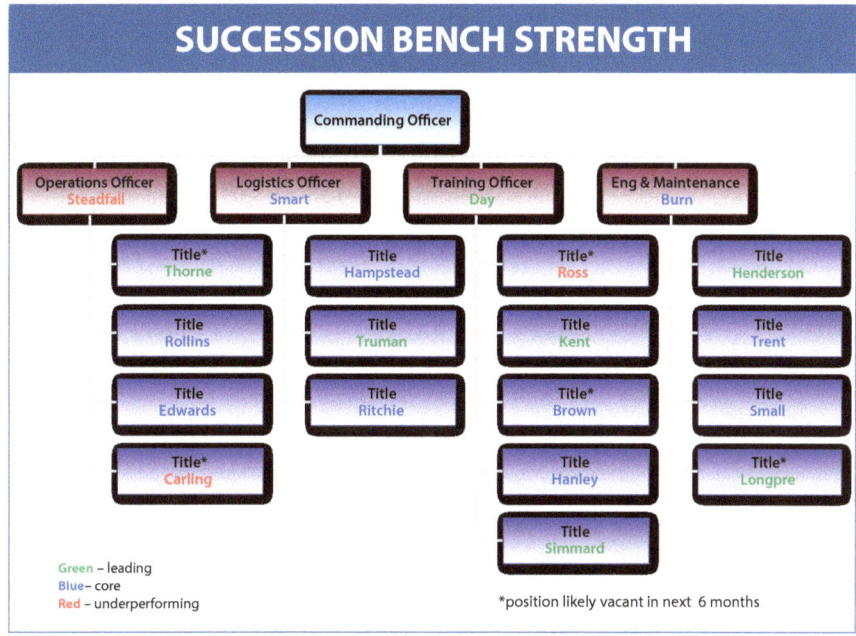

Figure 12 – Visual Bench Strength

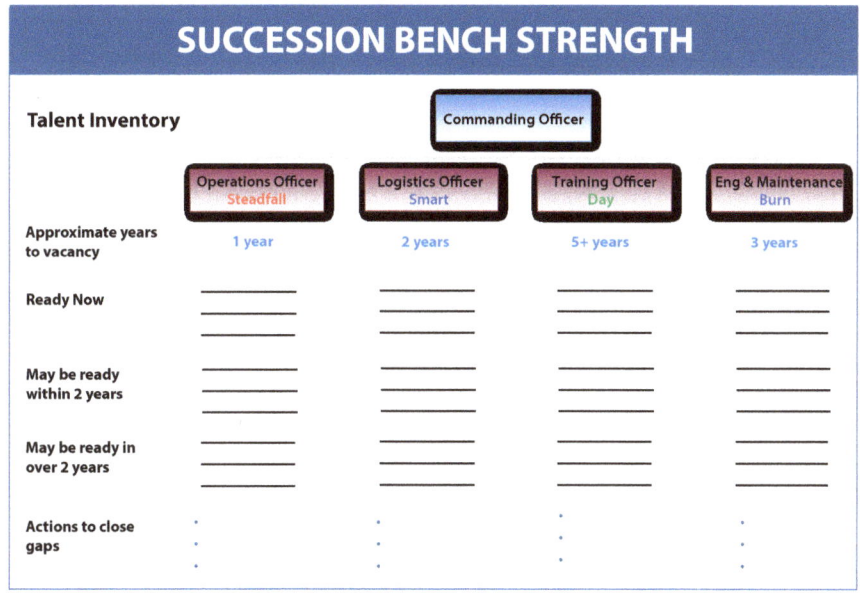

Figure 13 – Succession Talent Inventory

The critical learning that surfaced for me when I made the transition to the private sector (contrasting my military experience to that of the private sector) was that the performance management system we used in the Air Force was more heavily focused on dealing with succession and development than it ever was with underperformers. My observation in moving to the private sector was that performance management was far more focused on the "squeaky wheel," the underperformers, and that far too few conversations were devoted to identifying, developing, and retaining the strongest performers to become leaders for the future. Three very simple metrics can help you assess the utility and thoroughness of your succession considerations:

1. Reports: The completion rates of performance management documents for your work force—do we have an objective database from which to make decisions?

2. Attention: The time you and your senior leaders devote to reviewing performance across your workforce—do we really know and manage the most critical asset (people, especially the top performers)?

3. Depth: The number of people you have trained and ready to fill mission critical positions—do we have the depth of skills and knowledge we require in people for continuity and sustainability?

Large Versus Small

Small companies present an entirely different challenge when it comes to considering succession planning. Understandably, it's simply not possible to expand the depth chart when you've only just turned on the lights and opened the front doors. When virtually every single person is a 'one off' and you're struggling to generate cash flow and growth, succession planning is something that's a long way off. However, understanding the concepts and knowing that you need to grow and operate from a higher mindset before you can build it into your business will be critical to preparing you for continued success.

As you grow and develop as the CEO, in preparation for taking your business to higher levels, you'll constantly need to assess your staff and determine whether they currently possess or can rapidly develop the competencies needed to conduct business at the next level. In the same way that the Air Force would assess the "A Category" players to determine whether they'd be able to meet the demands they'd face at higher levels, you'll need to review and assess your staff to determine whether they can quickly adapt to the duties required several levels higher as well. An early entry person with strong generalist skills may not have the aptitude or the desire to adapt to the significant changes in complexity and job demands that will evolve as you grow your company.

> *"A company should limit its growth based on its ability to attract enough of the right people." – James C. Collins*

Through your growth and strategic planning processes it will be necessary to routinely identify the skills, knowledge, and competencies required for your company to succeed at the next level. While you should always demonstrate loyalty to the people who started the journey with you, you are doing a disservice to them and your growing company if you force them into positions where they're simply overwhelmed and fighting for survival. Invest in your employees early and invite them to reach the next level based on an understanding of the need for change and growth. Recognize, however, that unless they do grow or you can hire around them, that you're potentially accepting the creation of a bottleneck in your operations. As you contemplate hiring and training considerations, you should strive to create capacity with people that will be capable of running your business when it's three or four times its current size.

> *"The only thing worse than training your employees and having them leave, is not training them and having them stay." – Henry Ford*

CEO Development and Succession

Do not neglect yourself along this journey. It will be extremely important that you grow as a leader and as an entrepreneur if you're to stay ahead of the needs of your company. Unfortunately, a great many businesses fail because the leader is unable to grow at the pace required to stay ahead of the business. Surround yourself with strong advisers and consider finding a mentor or a coach. Recently, I had a conversation with a successful CEO who told me he'd had a leadership coach for himself and his executive team for the last few years. He commented on the tremendous difference it had made for his personal performance and that of the executive team as they interacted and worked to create sustainable excellence across their growing company. Given the improvements acknowledged, he marvelled somewhat at how few of his peer CEOs had taken similar steps.

There are lots of offerings on the market focused on CEO development that are worthy of your consideration. While their costs may often appear excessive when you're just starting out, the ability to learn from experienced peers, routinely be exposed to new and innovative ideas, and the ability to test your strategies and solutions to the problems you face will pay great dividends. This is not your practice life as a CEO and there are few opportunities for do-overs, so the benefits of coaching and CEO Mastermind groups are absolutely worthy of consideration.

> *"This is not your practice life as a CEO and there are few opportunities for 'Do-Overs', engage the wisdom and experience of others to mitigate the risks you'll undoubtedly face." – Jim Donihee*

In the corporate sector, CEO succession is the accountability of the Board of Directors. In smaller, private entrepreneurial entities that responsibility may well fall to you at the back end of your journey. For the CEO role especially, succession is a process and not an event—start it as soon as you begin thinking about your exit, especially if your retirement plan requires that you generate funds through the sale of your company. Absent a highly qualified, competent leader who's already in place, the sale may require that you remain anchored for an extended period of time to ensure continuity of the business and security of the proposed investment by the prospective buyer.

Building a sustainable organization will require that you travel the journey understanding the need for succession. At the outset you will not enjoy the luxury of a lot of bench strength. However, if you fix in your mind where you're going and identify the knowledge and capabilities that you will require further into the journey, you'll establish a strong path forward. Secure in that knowledge, you'll make good hires, decide on great promotions, and develop strong people capable of dealing with the growing complexities and challenges you will face.

Lessons drawn from the Air Force experience of this approach are often used by large corporations and applicable for you to consider. In short, as CEO you will need to be objective and transparent, fair and deliberate to ensure your succession practices hold a high degree of integrity. A strong, consistent performance management system that fairly identifies your future leaders and provides you with a clear snapshot of your bench strength will help you grow for the future and mitigate the risks that you face today. One of the biggest risks you will face as you grow is outpacing your human capacity to execute. Ensure that you invest in capacity, including your own, to avoid stumbling and forcing yourself into survival mode as you strive for the next stage in your growth.

SUMMARY POINTS

✓   Succession planning will ensure you are positioned to last.

✓   Succession options will largely be driven by the growth stage of your company:

     ○   In the early stages you'll be driven to the street, so hire thoughtfully.

     ○   Once your company is more mature, both the street and internal personnel will present options, so you should hire for competence and to reinforce your culture.

✓   A credible, trusted performance management system will be vital to successful succession planning.

✓   Differentiate your human resources based on their performance and their potential and spend more time on your best performers rather than the squeaky wheels. The former represents your future while the latter should be dealt with decisively.

✓   Simple visuals can provide powerful snapshots that depict the mission critical risks you face and the depth of personnel you have in development for the future.

✓   Don't neglect yourself—your continued growth and development is vital to ensure you stay ahead of the needs the organization.

ACTION POINTS

✓ Map your organization to assess the strength and depth of leadership to ensure continuity and sustainability.

✓ Assess the integrity of your performance management system—check the recommended metrics.

✓ Spend more time with your future leaders.

✓ Assess how you're investing in yourself.

9

PRINCIPLES OF WAR

"All men can see these tactics whereby I conquer, but what none can see is the strategy out of which victory is evolved." – Sun Tzu

Every so often we come across a set of principles that are timeless. The deep meaning and focus they bring to everything we do can provide a guiding light in the midst of the chaos and busyness that we experience in life. While the term "war" carries a terrible connotation for us all, as it should, we need to remember that the ultimate objective of war is peace. Man's experience over centuries of waging war has positioned us to draw some valuable principles, timeless principles, that can help focus us in our own journey. When given consideration in terms of building and growing our businesses, these timeless principles can provide many key insights.

Sun Tzu was a Chinese military strategist and a Taoist philosopher who lived around 300 BC. He was a highly successful general who is widely credited for writing *The Art of War*, which is one of the first scholarly works that set out principles for the conduct of war. His writings established that to wage war successfully required a coherent strategy, sound tactics, and practical doctrine dealing with intelligence, planning, command and control, execution, and administrative procedures. The clarity and applicability of these principles have stood the test of time since they were written some 2500 years ago and offer provocative focal points for consideration, both personal and as you strive to grow your business. These Principles of War have evolved and become more refined over centuries of combat operations and are now taught throughout all stages of leadership development in militaries around the world. Of late, they are also now taught in business schools in light of the valuable considerations they provide in planning and executing business operations focused on achieving the aim.

The principles authored by Sun Tzu hold great relevance, not only for professional militaries, but for business communities, companies, and individuals. Admittedly, in corporate or personal settings, you won't suffer the dire consequences of war in terms of having people perish. Still, when companies fail, people's livelihoods may perish, while their well-being and tremendous shareholder value can also be destroyed. For all of those reasons, a brief study of these powerful principles is warranted. See for yourself: what lessons can be drawn from them; how do they affect me personally; and, as I think about growing the business, what considerations emerge that I should reflect upon? When all is said and done, losing in business, just like losing in war, does not set the stage for longevity.

Business Impact

"Strategy without tactics is the slowest route to victory. Tactics without strategy is the noise before defeat." – Sun Tzu

I had just retired the from Canada's Air Force in August of 2000 when I joined the Alberta Energy Company (AEC). I had a fascinating role which involved creating communities of practice to spread knowledge and best operating practices across the company domestically and internationally. Throughout my years as an operational commander in Canada's military, serving both at home and abroad, I had become very familiar with the Principles of War and the clarity they provided for the planning and conduct of operations. The role I fulfilled for AEC allowed me the freedom of action to interact with expertise that ranged all away from the producing fields to leaders on the executive team, including the CEO. My experience as an operational commander leading large organizations was recognized and led me, from time to time, to engage in some very frank conversations with everyone I interacted with. What became evident to me, largely because of the growth of the company, was that many of the principles that had become so familiar to me were not being applied within the company.

I was fortunate because the CEO of AEC had served for a brief period as an honorary Colonel in the Canadian Air Force. While the role of an honorary Colonel is largely ceremonial in nature, that experience afforded him an opportunity to witness first-hand how our Air Force conducted operations. On more than one occasion, he had the opportunity to witness multinational operations from start to finish in terms of: how they were planned; how the strategy was executed; and how meaningful lessons were drawn from the operations through detailed After Action Reviews focused not on attributing blame, but on continuous improvement and the development of sustainable excellence. Because of this first-hand experience, he was highly receptive to the lessons that the Principles of War offered. The one-page briefing note that I prepared laid out the Principles of War and placed them in the context of the Alberta Energy Company's business operations. While that briefing note didn't become the bible for the conduct of operations, the CEO decided that there was sufficient focus and power in the document that he sent it to his entire executive cadre, as well as the members of the board of directors. I have since adapted that briefing note and used it to express the same powerful lessons while serving in senior executive roles at Canada's National Energy Board and, subsequently, while serving at the Canadian Energy Pipeline Association. In each of these instances, the Principles of War have provided a valuable construct to objectively question the way that current operations are being conducted and provide valuable insight into ways that business competitors or significant interest groups who oppose your operations will conduct themselves.

Personal Impact

"There are three constants in life . . . change,
choice, and principles." – Stephen Covey

The insights that the Principles of War provide at the corporate level are equally meaningful when you apply them through the lens of a personal level. If you give thought to yourself as a micro-corporation, you will quickly see the principles' relevance as they apply to yourself as you work to develop your competencies and build your business.

These invaluable principles, as they apply to the individual, are set out below. As you read them, do your best to reflect objectively on how they apply to you and what you can learn and do differently as a result.

Principles of War—
Applications to Personal Excellence and Competitive Advantage

PRINCIPLES OF WAR

A Background: The nine recognized *Principles of War* have evolved over centuries of combat operations and are now taught and reinforced to military commanders and leaders at all stages of their development. These principles are also widely recognized within the business world's competitive environment for their focus, simplicity, and potential to provide a guiding set of tenets leading to excellence in growth and execution. There is direct applicability of these tenets to personal growth and in the value they hold when planning for the growth of your company.

The Principles:

- Aim: *Selection and maintenance of the Aim—every military operation should be directed towards a clearly defined, decisive, and attainable objective.* Clearly define the aim of your activities and do not deviate from it. Retain your focus and consider your unique competencies. Consider opportunities that require the development of new competencies only if they originate from significant changes in the environment or present distinct and significant strategic or material value.

- Offensive: *Seize, retain, and exploit the initiative.* Maintain a deliberate, focused approach to your personal growth—employ the experience and knowledge you have gained to anticipate and prepare for emerging opportunities rather than reacting to the changing environment.

- Mass: *Mass the effects of overwhelming combat power at a decisive place and time.*

Apply your distinct knowledge and capabilities to establish a position of leadership in areas of your choice. Strategic external relationships and networks should be used to enhance your knowledge and skillsets, but *Force Majeur / Leadership positions* should remain the clear focus of your efforts and objectives.

- Economy of Force: *Employ all combat power available in the most effective way possible; allocate minimum essential combat power to secondary effort.* Enhance your ability to allocate finite resources, be they personal or financial, in a timely decisive manner. Improve the leverage of your expertise and improve your rapidity of action by developing standard processes and constantly improve by applying lessons learned without stifling innovation and decisiveness.

- Maneuver: *Place the enemy in a position of disadvantage through the flexible application of combat power.*
  Develop your strategies to obtain Leadership positions through the effective application of your core competencies. Take rapid, decisive action based on *Best Practice* processes and free and open exchange of knowledge and resources from across your networks to generate impact on opportunities.

- Unity of Command: *For every objective, seek unity of effort under one accountable commander.*
  You are accountable for your journey. You are either executing according to your plan or you are living according to someone else's plan. Hold yourself accountable for the objectives you set, reflect on the progress and outcomes you achieve, and hold yourself accountable to develop excellence as a habit.

- Security: *Never permit the enemy to acquire unexpected advantage.*
  Work hard to come to know yourself. Retain your objectivity, seek wise counsel, and believe in yourself. The most dangerous lies are the lies you tell yourself. Do not let the inner voices tied to your limiting beliefs serve as the enemy that will breed doubt and undermine you along your personal journey.

- <u>Surprise</u>: *Strike the enemy at a time or place or in a manner for which he is unprepared.*

  Your ability to gather information and learn in near real time across the entire breadth of opportunities will guide you to develop greater insights and awareness to the marketplace than ever before. As a leader focused on excellence you will need to focus your knowledge and expertise on rapidly emerging opportunities to develop and deliver excellent results and returns.

- <u>Simplicity</u>: *Prepare clear, uncomplicated plans and concise orders to ensure thorough understanding.*

  Your personal vision and objectives need to be defined with clarity and precision. Your strategy needs to be clear and unambiguous, and your actions need to align with your vision and constantly improve to create personal excellence.

SUMMARY POINTS

For many centuries military operations have been conducted with the ultimate aim of creating peace. Because the consequences of war are so very high, valuable lessons have been learned that are applicable to a multitude of scenarios. A brilliant Chinese general—Sun Tzu—was amongst the first to author principles that a set out strategy, tactics, and doctrine related to the conduct of wartime operations. Those principles adapted and refined throughout the centuries still offer powerful lessons that are studied by military leaders and business communities around the world.

These principles apply equally to you and to the growth and sustainability of your business.

- ✓ The Principles of War, refined over centuries of military operations, apply directly to how you grow your business.

- ✓ View yourself as a micro corporation, a company of one, and objectively explore how they can guide you more directly to achieve your personal vision.

ACTION POINTS

✓ Review the Principles of War, identifying where and why you deviate from them.

✓ Share the Principles of War with your leadership team and engage in discussions on how their application could improve your business.

✓ Engage your team members and say to them: "Tell me how applying the Principles of War would improve our business performance!"

10

ACCOUNTABILITY

"Accountability is the glue that ties commitment to results."
– Bob Proctor

Accountability is another one of those abstract concepts that will be instrumental to the success of the company you want to build. You can't reach out and touch accountability, but as you grow and the demands on you and your company begin to build up, you will know very quickly if there's a collective sense of accountability present across your company. It'll be reflected by things as simple as how people are greeted at your front door or things as complex as how your employees treat clients, execute their work, and honour interdependencies across teams and business units.

"You will get what you are willing to tolerate – that especially goes for accountability and performance. Set your bar high and reinforce it persistently". – Jim Donihee

Accountability is no different than any of the critical concepts we've discussed so far. You will get the level of accountability, the level of performance, that you are willing to tolerate. Along your journey, you won't be able to oversee or scrutinize every single transaction that takes place across the organization. For that reason, you'll need to develop a universal understanding of what "great" looks like, what constitutes exceptional service, and, especially, what constitutes "unacceptable." Your job as the CEO is to make sure that common understanding is pervasive throughout your organization. You'll need to ensure that common understanding is not ambiguous, and that conversations and practices routinely reinforce the standards you want to achieve—the What—and the expectations of how that will occur—the How. The foundation of accountability is a strong vision statement and consistent leadership that sets out clear priorities and value-based performance standards to bind everyone together.

You will set the tone for what accountability will mean in your company. If you approach accountability from the viewpoint that it's something that only rolls downhill, you will quickly foster a culture that invokes a "do as I say and not as I do" approach to leadership, relationships, and operations. That type of culture sets out a "blame game" and suppresses respectful challenge that is critical to learning, innovation, and continuous improvement. On the other hand, if you establish an approach to accountability wherein it flows in both directions, you'll elicit higher degrees of engagement, greater creativity and innovation, and better outcomes across the workforce. When accountability flows in both directions, it means the responsibilities for everyone are clearly defined. It is entirely legitimate for workers to hold expectations of their leaders that are at least as high as the leaders have of them. Importantly, it also means there are practices in place that provide for respectful and transparent review and learn sessions that are focused on improvement and free of hierarchy. Transparency, mutual accountabilities and a strong focus on continuous improvement foster high levels of trust and engagement.

> *"A culture of accountability makes a good organization great and a great organization unstoppable."* – Henry Evans

A culture of accountability doesn't mean that everyone is standing around waiting for the ax to fall. It does mean that there's an ease of operations, a coherency that ensures clarity around where everyone fits and how they're to perform their duties. So, what exactly are the key pieces required to create a culture of accountability?

Clarity of Understanding and Alignment: Clarity of understanding and alignment will be created through precise and effective communications, which you initiate. Starting with a clear understanding of your vision and the key strategic elements that are integral to how you will achieve that vision is necessary to ensure everybody knows where you're going. Having a clear understanding of the major milestones and deliverables sets the foundation for everyone to see where their unique contributions fit into the puzzle. Each level of leadership will need a clear understanding of the elements for which they are responsible, so they, in turn, can ensure their teams own and execute against the expectations delegated to them. Leaders, each in their own right, need to make sure that expectations are clear through open and transparent dialogue. Conversations and questions need to confirm everyone understands their mutual expectations, especially where there are shared resources, interdependencies, and the need for collaboration across organizational boundaries. If you conclude these conversations and employees are guessing what they're supposed to do, any mismatch between expectations and outcomes belongs to the leader.

"If the words of the commander are not clear and distinct, if orders are not thoroughly understood, then the general is to blame." – Sun Tzu

One tool that I used to ensure openness and transparency around the leadership team's expectations while I served as the Chief Operating Officer at Canada's National Energy Board was to post each of our performance contracts on the internal web site. By doing that, everyone in the organization could see the cascading nature of the tasks and deliverables that were required. Employees could see where they each fit in, and, perhaps most importantly, by understanding the expectations of each of their leaders and the interdependencies that existed between them, they could see that accountability didn't simply roll downhill. As we moved through the organization, they could easily understand how the various goals and deliverables became more granular in nature and eventually were expressed in their own individual performance contracts.

Leadership: Leaders are instrumental in establishing and sustaining a consistent culture of accountability throughout the organization. Leaders of every level set the tone by engaging with their workers to ensure they clearly understand what is expected of them and by providing the ongoing coaching and guidance that is necessary to deliver quality products. Leaders need to ensure effective allocation of resources and that their people are properly trained to perform their tasks.

In transitioning from the military to industry, one of the things I particularly noticed was the percentage of time each of those sectors devoted to training vs. operations. In the military, generally speaking, the consequences of failure are so high that tremendous amounts of time are devoted to training. Personnel were well trained and given responsibilities for which they were well prepared, especially as it pertained to leadership roles. In industry, however, I noted that strong technical leaders were often promoted and placed in managerial leadership roles for which they were ill-prepared. Although strong technically, prospective leaders often had neither the managerial nor leadership training required to assure their success. Training was often seen as a cost rather than an investment and the impact of poor leadership imposed a tremendous toll. Research has consistently shown that workers don't leave companies, they leave leaders. The cost of poor leadership generally results in pockets of attrition, diminished productivity and engagement, and inconsistencies in the otherwise coherent culture that you are working hard to establish.

Workers: Your workers will deliver the goods. They need to know what is expected of them in terms of quality and timeliness, and they need to know they're not simply a resource to blame when things go wrong. They need to know that they are full members of the team and that you, and every leader throughout the company, have their backs and care about their success as much as you do your own. Workers need to know and understand that there's a fair system of consequences that will recognize outstanding performance and deal consistently with poor performance for everyone concerned, including the leaders. Workers need to be engaged and feel safe to ensure they will ask questions to confirm their understanding of deliverables so they can fully own and execute on what is expected of them.

You need to understand that your workers are closest to the coalface and often identify innovations and solutions to make operations more effective. It's important for you, then, to actively create circumstances where their voices can be heard, and you can learn and benefit from their knowledge and experience. Creating communities where workers can actively share their challenges and solutions provides an excellent example of respecting them and harvesting their wisdom.

While serving as the Vice-President of Organizational Effectiveness at a major Oil & Gas company, we created forums that brought workers from common disciplines together from across the company for two-day retreats. Over the course of the two days, the CEO and members of the senior executive team would join them to provide an overview of the company and the major milestones that would stretch over the next year or two. This provided the workers with direct contact to the senior leaders and, more importantly, it provided them with a clear understanding of where the company was going, the challenges that the executive team faced, and a valuable opportunity for a frank and open Q&A.

What always delivered tangible results over those two days, however, was the opportunity for the workers to share amongst themselves their greatest wins and challenges. Invariably someone's win would match up against another's challenge and needed improvements. The forums created a unique opportunity where innovations were quickly disseminated to enhance operations. At the minimal cost to conduct these forums, tangible outcomes were reflected through many hundreds of thousands of dollars (sometimes millions) in efficiencies, a much deeper understanding of where the company was going, and a much stronger community of expertise with greater engagement and accountability to deliver. These forums, conducted across a number of key operational disciplines, had a tremendous impact on increasing respect and on strengthening a culture of accountability. We'll talk more about it as we progress throughout our journey, but these forums highlighted three key principles to achieving excellence within teams: affinity, reality, and communications. Affinity relates to whether there is a true sense of community across the team, business unit, or organization. How strongly we care about one another and want to contribute to each other's success is increased through affinity. Reality revolves around having a shared and objective understanding of the state of play. Finally, communications, and whether they can get well below the water's surface to be frank and honest, provides the vehicle through which that shared sense of reality is created and the community can be engaged to generate improvements.

After Action Reviews (AAR)—Focused on Continuous Improvement: Learning, adapting, and innovation will be key to creating and sustaining your competitive advantage. Those factors all lead to continuous improvement, which is a key discipline to inculcate into your company. To ensure those outcomes fall into place takes discipline, and while it takes time to contrast the results you achieved and why you achieved them against what you aimed for, that's the essential ingredient to continuous improvement.

Review and learn debriefs (AARs) are part of the DNA that we are raised on in the military, and they're instrumental to achieving peak performance and mission accomplishment. After every flying mission I was ever part of, the pilots and key support staff would conduct a detailed mission debrief that drew out lessons learned with the sole intention of improving the effectiveness of operations. Irrespective of seniority, all were held to the same high standard of performance and lessons were identified through open, frank conversation free of any blame.

Review and learns, when part of your DNA and conducted effectively, will make the difference between a sustainable business and failure. Review and learns don't need to be cumbersome and overly time consuming. Here are some key principles essential to ensuring their effectiveness:

- Results, not blame—conversations are focused on what occurred and how to improve upon it, not on who to blame.

- Open and honest discussion—rank / hierarchy must be left at the door to invite open and frank discussion of what transpired.

- Everyone participates—everyone's experience of the events is important to fully explore what transpired and to learn. The tone and approach must be inclusive with everyone held to the same standard of performance.

- Continuous improvement—lessons need to be identified and shared to retain what went well and to improve upon, within established timelines, what did not.

The actual conduct of the review and learn primarily hinges off four key questions:

1. What did we expect to happen—was the mission (the intended outcome) along with any secondary missions clear?

2. What actually happened—what outcome did we get as it relates to the primary or any secondary missions?

3. What went well and why?

   a. What results do we want to retain?

   b. What do we need to do to ensure those results are sustained (planning, equipment, logistics, training, personnel)?

4. What can be improved and how?

    a. Was the primary mission clearly defined and understood by all—were any secondary missions identified, and, if so, were they equally well defined and understood?

    b. Were everyone's roles, priorities, and accountabilities clear?

    c. What assumptions about execution were made that did not support clean execution?

    d. Were the plan and timings clear, realistic, and well briefed?

    e. What happened during execution that affected the intended outcome?

        i. Unanticipated circumstances / poor business intelligence— were there flaws in the planning process that failed to anticipate business intelligence, timing, personnel, technical, or logistical requirements.

        ii. Training or knowledge deficiency—were personnel properly trained and all standards adhered to for the roles they were to execute.

        iii. Equipment or logistics deficiency—were the equipment / technical and support requirements adequate and timely.

        iv. Command and control, leadership, or communications deficiencies—did everyone act in accordance with the plan and standards of operations expected; what can be learned/adopted or improved upon.

    f. Whose accountability is it to develop and implement the identified improvements and by when?

<u>After Action Review—A Case in Point</u>: The culture you tolerate within the organization will have a direct impact on whether your organization learns and improves, or whether you repeat costly errors and, potentially, the loss of life that can accompany them. In this particular case in point, I was invited to assist a small aviation firm to conduct an internal review of how it conducted operations following an aircraft crash that resulted in the loss of three lives. In working specifically with the aircrew, which included the aircraft captains and the first officers, it rapidly became clear that open and honest communications could not take place with both groups in the same room. The culture that existed throughout their flying operations was such that the first officers had very little say and

were often silenced by the aircraft captains. That reality led to challenges in crew coordination, which induced significant risks throughout the flying operations, and diminished any opportunity for continuous improvement. Clearly the guideline surrounding "no rank or hierarchy in the room in order to facilitate a frank and open After Action Review" was not being followed, and the trust and potential for learning was severely impaired. In this case, in order to move forward, I ended up separating the two groups to draw out each group's lessons, after which I brought them back together and facilitated the exchange of information. Going forward, the company set out to change the culture in the cockpit to make maximum use of the knowledge of both aircraft captains and first officers, so as to increase its safety of operations. The point in this short vignette is that the value of After Action Reviews will very largely be determined by the levels of trust, safety and openness of communications permitted. The discussions must be free of blame, address all participants equally and be centered around the sole purpose of continuous improvement.

The Language of Accountability: The language that becomes prevalent throughout your organization provides a window to your culture's soul and how you execute operations. If you listen carefully, you'll quickly gain clear insights into the attitudes and engagement levels that everyone exhibits. You will quickly be able to discern where they reside on the ladder of accountability (see graphic) and whether they are making a positive or negative net contribution to your culture of accountability. Are people hanging out as victims who are resistant to change and abdicating ownership of their outcomes, or do they have a leadership mindset that is focused on learning and adapting to tackle the challenges of the future? Once you have a chance to assess where your workforce is hanging out on the ladder collectively, you can actively engage in various tactics to climb to and sustain your position at the top of the ladder of accountability.

Remember, you will get the level of accountability that you are willing to tolerate. Climbing the ladder of accountability requires leadership and motivation, not blame and dismissals.

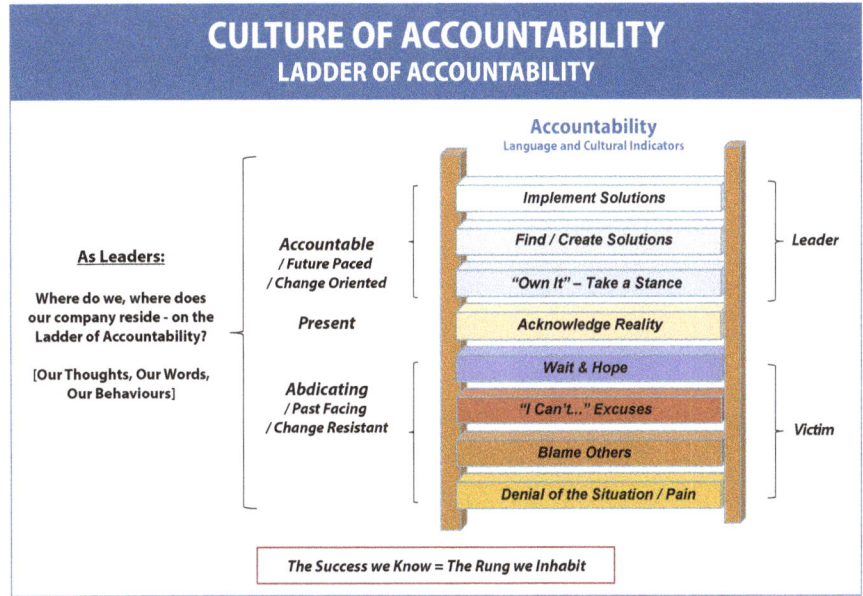

Figure 14 – Ladder of Accountability

<u>Dyads—Powerful Insights</u>: Getting and sustaining your position at the top, or amongst the top businesses will take consistent efforts that begin with you and the executive team members. You set the tone, and the example that your team provides will absolutely induce waves throughout the organization. A simple and yet extremely effective tool that I've used with executive teams is the conduct of dyads of inquiry.

A dyad exercise provides a powerful connection between you and your executive team members (any team for that matter), which will provide extremely valuable insights into how you can increase your effectiveness. During this exercise, which might last an hour depending on the size of your executive team, each of you will spend a few minutes paired off with each member of the team. During the exchanges that occur, each of you will pose a question to which the other person responds. Your response to them can only be "Thank You" or perhaps "Clarify." The aim of the exercise, which is highly impactful, is to deepen connection and to express constructive statements to enhance performance. The exchange is not a dialogue, and because there are no "ya but's" or immediate feedback provided, the exchanges rapidly become very frank and powerful. Four examples of dyad instructions that would have a dramatic impact on you and your executive team might be:

1. Tell me how I can be a more effective member of our executive team.

2. Tell me how I can better support you in achieving your goals.

3. Tell me where our accountabilities are breaking down.

4. Tell me where our culture is impacting our success.

Culture of Accountability—Its Impact

As previously discussed (in chapters 3 and 4), your company will have a culture. The real question, then, is whether the culture that is showing up is the one you want. Is your culture making the highest possible contribution to your collective success? Is it a culture that is wedded in excuses and looks for people to blame, or is it a culture that is focused on learning and continuous improvement? Are you and your leaders actively listening to the language of your culture, especially as it relates to accountability, and looking to up-level it?

You will learn, as the size and diversity of your company grows, that the main way for you to positively influence your operations is through the creation of a high-performance culture with a clear focus on accountability and continuous improvement. Setting out to build and instill it right from the outset will save you a lot of grief when you get further downstream.

> *"The culture of any organization is shaped by the worst behaviour the leader is willing to tolerate." – Gruenter and Whitaker*

SUMMARY POINTS

✓ You will get the level of accountability that you are willing to tolerate.

✓ Clear accountabilities for all establish mutual expectations and disable the "blame game."

✓ Posting executive performance contracts provides transparency, and clarity of accountabilities and interdependencies.

✓ Training related to leadership and accountability is a vital investment, not a cost.

✓ Workers frequently know the answers to the toughest challenges—trust them and create opportunities for them to collaborate and innovate.

✓ After Action Reviews should be part of your organizational DNA.

✓ The Language of Accountability prevalent in your organization provides a window to the soul of your company.

✓ Dyads will provide powerful insights that will heighten your and your leaders' effectiveness.

ACTION POINTS

✓ Reflect on what you're tolerating and why.

✓ Increase the transparency of executive accountabilities.

✓ Train your leaders to strengthen your culture and accountability.

✓ Review your After-Action processes and how systemically they're used to improve performance.

✓ Use dyads to strengthen your team and its performance.

11

BOUNDARIES TO SUCCESS: BOUNDARYLESS EXECUTION

"Today's organizations must become
Boundaryless if they are to be successful."
– Jack Welch

Success and growth will present many challenges. Inevitably, size and scale will introduce complexity in your organization and, if you're not careful, it will be easy to lose sight of who you are competing with. Throughout my career in the military, I had the opportunity to work in and lead many large organizations. The things I was always clear about throughout that time was who the enemy was, what the mission was, and who the friendly forces were to ensure that we won as a team comprised of many parts. Regardless of the various forces assigned to complete the mission, there was an absolute understanding that winning depended entirely on a sharp and constant focus on excellence in execution, and high expectations of each other in terms of collaboration and mutual support.

For you, too, excellence in execution has to be a fundamental tenet of your culture. Regardless of how many teams you bolt together, it will be imperative that they work together to collaborate, eliminate surprises, and to succeed. There are a lot of levers in play to ensure the interactions between teams, business units, and divisions can be focused on the free and open exchange of knowledge and operating practices in order to rapidly migrate lessons learned, innovations, and success. That exchange focused on excellence and execution will require, as you grow your business, that you strive for community, collaboration, and trust while precluding the development of competitive silos within your business.

In effect, while serving in the military, it didn't matter which team you were on, squadron you were flying with, or country you were from; we all wore the same badge on our shoulders and were focused on winning. Imagine my surprise, when transitioning from Canada's Air Force to the Oil & Gas industry, that I found, even within a relatively small company, the competition between business units frequently created barriers to sharing knowledge and executing the best way possible for the good of the entire company. Competition for capital, rewards and recognition systems, compensation structures, and unbridled egos often reinforced behaviours that did not serve the best interests of the company or its shareholders. As you grow and develop your company, then, it will be vitally important to consider how you want your culture to evolve.

"We don't rise to the level of our expectations; we fall to the level of our training." – Archilochus

Military Training—Models of Value

Canada has long conducted a major multi-national flying training exercise called MAPLE FLAG. This large live flying exercise, routinely involving well over 5000 personnel and up to 100 aircraft from several countries, provided an excellent case in point for the exchange of knowledge and excellence of execution. Operational analysis and history have demonstrated to us that the heaviest losses in combat generally occur during the first ten wartime sorties of a pilot's life. Exercise MAPLE FLAG, therefore, was created to replicate the complexity and chaos of those first ten missions.

Air forces from around the world would converge on the air force base in Cold Lake, Alberta every summer in order to train in the most realistic conditions possible. The air weapons range where the training took place afforded the ability to fly missions involving large numbers of aircraft against opposing forces, replicating the types and tactics of both the air and ground defense forces they would face. These missions, often involving upwards of a hundred aircraft, could be recorded in three dimensions from start to finish. The simulated enemy forces were schooled and practiced in the enemy tactics that were anticipated in the event of any kind of conflict and provided invaluable training as our new pilots flew missions against them. The true value that the pilots and crews derived over the course of the six-week exercise resulted from three distinct aspects:

1. Planning Conditions—they were able to plan missions under realistic conditions that replicated the demanding scenarios they would face in real time (tight timelines, deployed operations, capable enemies, and interoperability in multinational forces).

2. Airspace—they were able to fly in a vast airspace that accurately replicated conditions they would face in wartime operations. Aircrews could fly up to supersonic airspeeds from ground level to infinity against aircraft and ground defence systems simulating enemy tactics and weapons capabilities.

3. After Action Reviews (AAR)—most importantly, the instrumented recording capabilities of the air weapons range supported detailed AARs that provided for complete transparency in how plans were executed along with rapid and effective exchange of lessons learned without boundaries. Crews could rapidly see what worked and what didn't work, and they embraced the need to share lessons. The bottom line is that the need to survive creates an enormously powerful community. Furthermore, the AAR provided an effective forum to evaluate:

   a. Planning: were the plans effective; were they based on best knowledge of enemy tactics and technology; were they effectively briefed and understood; were they realistic based on our own competencies and technology.
   b. Execution: how did we execute; what changed and why did things change once we got into the air; and, especially, how could we do better on the next round in terms of planning, tactics, training, and technology.

To ensure the effectiveness of the AAR processes some particularly important cultural tenets were always stressed:

1. Park your rank and your ego at the door—rank and ego have no place in the conversation when you're focused on learning and achieving the best possible execution.

2. Humility and transparency—the need for open uninhibited conversation cannot be overstated if you're focused on identifying the lessons and

improving performance. It's not about blame; it's about identifying lessons and improving performance.

3. Boundaryless execution—the endgame of achieving the best possible execution for everyone involved, requires rapidly identifying and promulgating the lessons learned without being constrained by organizational boundaries or internal competition that may evolve in your company.

The major difference between the military or any professional sports team in comparison to your company is the luxury of dedicating significant amounts of time to training. In the military it's likely that about 80% of your time will be spent training for that 20% of the time when you're called upon to conduct live operations. Second best in military operations is simply not good enough because the cost in terms of lives and equipment is simply too high. In contrast to the military, your company will likely be conducting operations at least 90% of the time because the cost of downtime and training can significantly impact the bottom line. At the same time, however, the cost of repetitive mistakes, impediments to innovation, and suboptimal execution across various units in your organization can weigh very heavily on your profitability and, ultimately, your survival as a viable company.

"Do the best you can until you know better. Then when
you know better, do better." – Maya Angelou

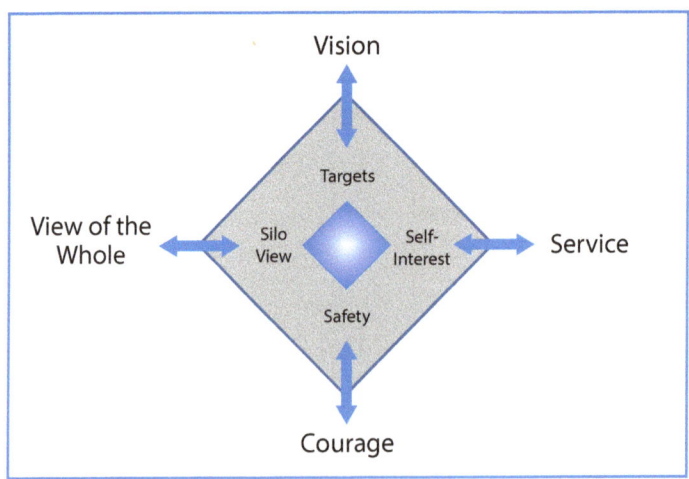

Figure 15 – Tactical to Strategic Success

Your role as CEO is to create the conditions where the forces to excel as an individual / sub-unit are in balance with the need to ensure the most effective execution of operations at the organizational level. For that reason, as depicted above, it's important to create a culture where collaboration and execution at the corporate level thrive over self-interest, silos, and individual targets.

> *"Learn all you can from the mistakes of others. You won't*
> *have time to make them all yourself." – Anonymous*

Company Model—Community of Practice

One of the models we created and used very effectively inside one company I worked at was the intentional creation of communities of practice (CoPs). While there were numerous common functions existing within different business units, there were no mechanisms in place to bring the practitioners together in order to share and learn from one another. As a result, their behaviours were principally aligned on individual targets inside their vertical silos of operations. The costs to the company were significant, either in terms of opportunity costs because innovations and improved operating practices were not being shared, or because mistakes and painful lessons were being replicated in various areas of the company.

So, to counteract the silo-based view, we set up some simple off-sites where we brought all of the practitioners together. Our aim was to create a network founded on trust and safety, with the deeper understanding of the company's vision and expectations, as well as how we could be in service to one another rather than being fixed on self-interest. The forums were focused not on leaders and managers necessarily but on the practitioners in some of the largest cost-related functions of how the company did business. In this case, it was an Oil & Gas company, so separate forums were held for key disciplines such as: drilling operations, supply chain operations, gas plant operations, and geology and geophysical operations. As a simple lead-in to the forums, we would canvass each of the participants and prepare a detailed binder that would outline their key areas of expertise, identify their most recent innovation or operational improvement, and also identify their most burning challenge. Invariably some attendees had already solved challenges faced by their peers and others had introduced operational improvements or technologies that when widely adopted offered savings of hundreds of thousands if not millions of dollars.

Some of the significant benefits of these forums were:

1. Creating networks and trust—the opportunity to come to know one another and to work on a personal level over a few days meant that silos were being dismantled and the participants would pick up the phone to ask for or to help one another going forward.

2. Community Web Pages—CoP web pages were created, which provided a means of ongoing connection and communication in support of collaboration and innovation going forward.

3. Identifying wins—problems were solved, and valuable wins were identified that could immediately be put into practice. Conservative estimates routinely identified many hundreds of thousands, if not millions of dollars in savings from each forum.

4. Strategic view—the forums presented an opportunity for the CEO and key executive team members to provide a strategic overview of the company and reinforce the values of teamwork and service that crossed vertical silos.

The challenge with boundaries that you'll face as your organization grows is recognizing they are forming walls that need to be dismantled to ensure knowledge can flow with the speed and flexibility needed to survive in a highly competitive business environment. The barriers can show up in your hierarchy where it's perceived that knowledge is power, across teams or business units that are strongly incented to achieve individual results absent a corporate view, or due to geographically dispersed operating entities. Your challenge will be to ensure that you retain the proper balance between sustaining a meritocracy, within which individuals need to be developed and recognized, while ensuring that everyone understands the company vision and maintains a view of the whole—to be in service to one another to collaborate and achieve the overarching goals of the company.

SUMMARY POINTS

✓ Excellence in execution demands focused leadership and a culture that eliminates boundaries.

✓ Silos and internal competition can create destructive barriers to organizational success.

✓ Careful attention to the cultural levers: communications, performance expectations, and rewards and recognition systems will have a definite impact on how boundaries show up in your organization.

✓ Make the most of the training opportunities and reinforce them with systemic After Action Review processes to identify and promulgate lessons learned focused on improving operations.

✓ Successful After Action Reviews require transparency, honesty, and that rank and egos are left at the door.

✓ Communities of Practice can be invaluable to strengthen trust-based networks and identify wins that traverse organizational boundaries.

ACTION POINTS

✓ Review the operating practices of your company in search of boundaries to the flow of knowledge, innovation, and excellence in operations.

✓ Assess your compensation practices to ensure you're not suffering unintended consequences, such as holding back on sharing knowledge due to internal competition.

✓ Assess your After Action Review processes to ensure they drive learning and continuous improvement at the organizational level.

12

COMMS 1—GET THE WORD OUT

*"Communication is the fuel that ignites and
sustains the passion and drive for your workforce
to achieve great things."*
– Jim Donihee

No matter how brilliant your technology or the quality of service you provide, that alone will not be enough. As you start and grow your company, your ability to communicate will set the stage for the continued success you want to achieve. As your business expands and complexity increases, success will forever elude you unless you are able to ignite the passion and align the various elements of your workforce. Imagine for a moment a customer that experiences several touchpoints from your company and the confusion that would arise if the approach, quality, and processes were different in each instance. It calls up the visual of an octopus whose eight arms are completely disconnected, each serving its own unique purpose rather than being aligned and focused on the well-being of the whole.

Your objective as the CEO will be to communicate and ensure those many arms act as the various instruments of a symphony. They need to be in complete harmony, acting on a consistent set of values and a common mission and purpose focused and dedicated to the results you need to achieve.

In the early days, you'll likely either be doing it all (planning, executing, communicating), or will at least have a hand in how it's all being done. As the size and complexity of your business grows, however, you will become increasingly dependent on the actions of others to execute your business plan. Communications will be key to getting everyone on the same page and establish unity of purpose as a foundation for operations across your company.

"Communication is the essential ingredient to a shared understanding of the reality you want to create versus what you are currently experiencing – what is, what's needed and how it's to be achieved." – Jim Donihee

Communications Template—Simple Model

The use of some simple models can help clarify your thinking while also providing useful building blocks to structure the development and execution of your communications. The following template is widely used and provides an effective start point from which to grow forward.

SIMPLE COMMUNICATIONS PLAN TEMPLATE	
Objective	What's the overall goal—what do you want your audience to know, what do you want them to do?
Audience	Who is the audience—what do you know about their values and attitudes, and how best to influence their actions?
Hearts & Minds	What do you want them to feel—how do you want to influence the beliefs and attitudes they currently hold?
Key Messages	What few, simple key messages will achieve your objective?
Where & How	Where and how will you deliver your messages (physical locations, in person or via others, technology or print media)?
Timing, Resources, Accountabilities	When do you execute the plan? How frequently will you deliver the key messages? What budget and resources (personnel / IT / logistics) are required to execute the plan? Who is accountable for approving the messages and executing the plan?
Measurement / Validation	How do you plan to measure the effectiveness of the communications plan (mid-course / afterwards)? How do you measure the shift in attitudes? How do you measure the accomplishment of the actions that you wanted your audience to take?

Table 7 – Simple Communications Template

The Approach in Practice—Communications Through a Merger

*"The goal is to provide inspiring information that creates
community and moves people to action." – Guy Kawasaki*

One of the most powerful examples of a well-executed communications plan that I worked on dealt with the merger of two major entities involving several thousand personnel. As is always the case, there was considerable anxiety across the two work-forces relating to who would be winners and losers as the merger was consummated. In this instance, as with all mergers, it was important to move thoughtfully, yet swiftly to develop and execute a communications plan that would settle the workers. The cultures of the two organizations were significantly different prior to the merger, consequently establishing the cultural norms going forward was a critical task to be completed. Communications was to play a vital role in making this happen.

The CEO created a small strategic task force that operated against a very tight timeline. Its goal was to listen to the concerns across the entire workforce and assist the CEO in drafting the key materials necessary to execute a strategic communications plan that would create community and reset the organization's culture going forward. Given the size and scale of the newly merged entity, the CEO knew that a culture of excellence would be essential to achieve the full business potential that the merger offered.

With the assistance of the task force, the CEO set about authoring the single overarching document that would articulate the fabric for the new culture. He dubbed of the document the Corporate Constitution and it quickly evolved into a focused, concise document that articulated the key tenets of the new company. Although the combined workforces were the primary target audience, it was also well understood that the Corporate Constitution would be taken up by market analysts to assess the resolve and effectiveness of merging these two complex entities. As the document neared completion, it was reviewed and enhanced by both the newly formed executive team as well as the Board of Directors, but it always remained the CEO's document.

The Corporate Constitution articulated the vision, values, and behavioural expectations that every single employee would be held accountable to. It was rich with examples of what were and what were not the expectations and acceptable behaviours for all employees. The document, while powerful in its own right, needed to be supported by an effective communication and roll out plan to greatly enhance its impact in defining the go-forward culture.

Although it was a complex, highly orchestrated communications and roll out, using the simplified template that we looked at earlier will provide good insight into how it was executed:

EXAMPLE—MERGER CULTURAL COMMUNICATIONS	
Objective	• Ensure rapid establishment of the go-forward culture of excellence for the merged entity
Audience(s)	• Primary: all employees and contractors of the merged entity • Secondary: investors and market analysts
Hearts & Minds	• All members of the primary audience will have a deep understanding of the go-forward culture, especially as it relates to the mutual accountabilities they should exhibit and hold for one another.
Key Messages	• Detailed in the Corporate Constitution—culture of excellence is dependent on mutual accountabilities and the highest of expectations in a meritocracy.
Where & How	• CEO led, workforce-wide • Company-wide Town Hall, simulcast to field and international offices • CEO explains the Corporate Constitution and, shaking hands, personally hands a copy to each member of the executive team. • Executive team will, in turn, cascade the handshake and a copy of the document to their respective leaders and eventually through to every employee in the company. • Symbology: cascading handshake represents the mutual contract and accountability between all employees.
Timing, Resources, Accountabilities	• Launch Date—time and date TBD • X thousand copies of the Corporate Constitution—one per employee / contractor • Logistics (TV, IT, Venues, etc.) • Within one week of launch date, every leader is to have met with his / her team to have discussed and responded to questions regarding the Corporate Constitution
Measurement / Validation	• All employees have received the document • Employee survey to examine understanding • Annual cultural survey to validate implementation • Reactions from suppliers / analysts and shareholders

Table 8 – Sample Communications Plan

The rollout of the Corporate Constitution was well executed and while some commented on the elements of theatrics related to the handshakes and passing of the documents, there was no doubt in anyone's minds about the CEO's intentions or expectations regarding accountability. Within about two weeks of the launch date, every employee had received his or her copy from their supervisor and the die was cast for the go-forward culture of excellence. In the months that followed, the Corporate Constitution became a foundational document that underpinned leadership training, communications, and performance management as it evolved in the company.

Communications will be a key determinant in the success of your business. Your ability to communicate and awaken the passion in others will have a huge impact on whether you can attract investors and the talented employees you will need to grow your business. It's important to recognize that you are always communicating, whether it be through the words you choose, your body language, or your facial expressions. How you listen and respond to the input or questions of others also has a huge impact on the effectiveness of your communications. Like so many other things, the ability to communicate is a skill that will improve if you're willing to seek feedback and work at it.

SUMMARY POINTS

- ✓ Communications will be key to the success that you'll achieve throughout the lifespan of your business.

- ✓ As your business grows, your ability to lead and influence success will become increasingly dependent on your skills as a communicator.

- ✓ Simple templates, such as the example provided, can help you clarify your thinking and provide a structured approach to executing a viable communications plan.

- ✓ The words, the manner in which they are expressed, and, at times, the symbology surrounding the communications will be key to achieving the impact you intended.

✓ Communications will have a dramatic impact on the culture of your organization—clarity and consistency across your leadership team, especially, will be a barometer for cohesiveness and effectiveness.

ACTION POINTS

✓ Communicate actively to foster a shared understanding of vision, strategy and operational expectations.

✓ Seek feedback and coaching to continuously improve your communications.

13

COMMUNICATIONS 2—
MAKE IT PERSONAL, MAKE IT AUTHENTIC

"When you're communicating to win over
hearts and minds, it is far more important to be authentic,
to be real, than it is to be profound."
– Jim Donihee

I distinctly remember that morning. I got up early because I was preparing to take command of 410 Tactical Fighter Squadron, Canada's CF-18 Operational Training Squadron. I was sweating bullets because I knew I would be called upon to give a brief speech upon assuming command. While I had given hundreds of speeches and taught countless lessons, this was the first time I would stand in front of some 350 people as their commander. I felt compelled to say something really profound to set the course for the months that would follow. In the end, I spoke authentically from my heart about who I was, how much I trusted their expertise, and what I believed we could achieve by serving together, by serving each other. Those few minutes of openness and authenticity ended up being far more profound than "profound" could ever have been.

"The greatest problem in communication is the illusion that
it has been accomplished." – George Bernard Shaw

So exactly how do you break through the illusion that communication has taken place? If the entire purpose of communications is to ensure that you reach a common understanding of the messages needed to achieve your goals, you have to work at understanding the filters and biases that shape the exchange for both sender and receiver. Your ability to recognize and work through the filters and biases that you come up against, including your own, will shape the success that you achieve.

Neurolinguistic programming (NLP) provides an excellent foundation on which to quickly examine the process of communications. As CEO and leader of the organization, it is your accountability to ensure that everyone gets on the same page. As you receive information and see and hear events going on around you, they are interpreted through a complex set of filters that have developed throughout your lifetime. For example, some of the more powerful filters that influence you will be:

- Values and Beliefs—values and beliefs are shaped principally through the first decade of your life. The schooling that you received, religious practices and faith within which you were raised, and family dynamics and culture are all proven to have a significant impact on the shaping of our values and beliefs.

- Memories and Experiences—memories and experiences have a tremendous influence on creating the filters that evolve not only in the workplace, but throughout our lives. For example, when a leader encourages you to speak freely and then jumps on you when you express something challenging, you will remember that and certainly refrain from speaking out again in the future.

- Language—certain words or phrases may carry a very heavy charge for some individuals, while being completely acceptable to others. Ensuring that ground rules are in place to request clarification or point out the charged phrases are invaluable conditions to effective communications.

These examples of filters as well as several others depicted in the following graphic all come into play in order to create an internal representation of the events or communication you are receiving. What is always critical as a senior leader, especially as an executive leader, is to assess what you are receiving and then to meaningfully choose your response. Being fully present in the moment and seeking to understand will permit you to be reflective rather than reactive, and will lead to far more effective communications.

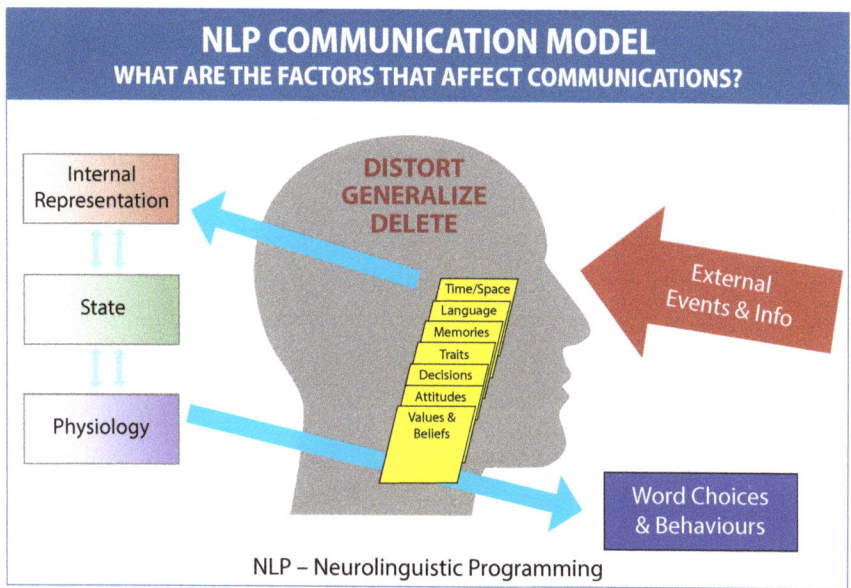

Figure 16 – NLP Communications Model

During the early growth stages of your company, this whole communications process can be pretty simple when the headcount is very small. As you add more people, and especially when you reach the point where you need to communicate through others, the layer upon layer of filters that come into play can greatly dampen the clarity and effectiveness of communications. In face-to-face communications, research indicates that as much as 93% of communication effectiveness results from tone of voice and body language. Those numbers are staggering and should strongly reinforce the value of face-to-face communications in your mind. If you really want to understand what your people are thinking, and, even more importantly, if you really want them to understand what you were thinking, there is no substitute for face-to-face. Clearly, in-person opportunities become more difficult as the company grows, however, there can still be a number of ways for you to listen to their views and get a message out in person.

Communications—Invested in Turn-Around, Alignment, and Performance

When I first took over the role as the Chief Operating Officer (COO) of Canada's National Energy board, I was shocked to see how caustic the culture was and how guarded the communications were between frontline workers and the executive leadership. For several years, the organization had been led from the viewpoint of "do as I say and not as I do," which resulted in high levels of mistrust and cynicism. Over the next three years, a significant investment in communications as the language of leadership very significantly increased trust levels, engagement, and organizational performance.

As we saw from the NLP diagram, the behaviours and word choices routinely employed by members of the workforce provided a window to the soul of the organization. Behaviours and word choices painted a picture of a workforce that was risk averse and unable to speak its truth in terms of the stresses and challenges it was facing. For the next several months, we instituted, amongst others, the following communications and leadership focused activities:

- Coffee with COO—on a biweekly basis, I instituted what we called "Coffee with COO." These sessions lasted from 1 to 1 ½ hours and consisted of meetings with staff from all areas the organization. The meetings had no particular agenda other than an open and free exchange of information, and there were no intermediate leaders or HR staff present other than myself. The meetings primarily achieved two very significant outcomes:

  - They presented me an opportunity to listen intently to understand where members of the workforce were coming from—to gain an understanding of their reality; and

  - They presented an opportunity for workers to come to know me and the depth of my commitment as a leader to serve them, improve the culture, and facilitate their success.

Initially trust was low, cynicism was high, and workers were reluctant to attend. However, over time, the discussions became very open, frank, and highly productive.

- Vision and values—we refreshed the vision and values, especially as it pertained to appropriate behaviours and the accountabilities, we should all expect another. Reinforcing the accountabilities of leadership significantly altered the organization's tone because rather than an unquestioned top-down approach, it became clear that leaders too would be held to account.

- Leaders forum—we instituted a Leaders' forum that focused on open and frank exchanges to build a common understanding of where we were going and how we were going to get there. The forum sometimes involved off-sites so we could strengthen the social dynamics between leaders and get away from the formal environment of the workplace. In the preceding years, few efforts had been expended on leadership development; consequently, these forums were a big step forward on that front.

- Town Halls—Town Halls provided a valuable opportunity to meet with either the entire organization or various business units. While discussing progress and challenges, the aim of these meetings was to very publicly set out expectations in terms of what we were going to achieve and how we were going to achieve it.

- Leadership team performance contracts—annually, once the performance contracts for the leadership team were concluded, I ensured they were published on the corporate intranet. The contracts did not disclose any personal development objectives for the various leaders, however, they clearly articulated organizational performance objectives highlighting the interdependencies that existed between the various areas. Having visibility to the Executives' performance contracts locked in accountabilities and the need to honour interdependencies substantially increased trust across the organization.

- Ask COO—we provided an e-mail forum that permitted employees to anonymously ask questions of the COO. There was a lot of debate about whether the emails could be submitted anonymously or whether the sender should self-identify. In the end, while encouraging identification, I decided that because trust levels were so low, we would accept anonymous submissions. This tool provided many useful suggestions to improve policies and procedures. As time went on and the atmosphere changed, senders self-identified more frequently, which was an indication of increasing trust levels.

This array of touchpoints that were used over the course of a couple years afforded me the opportunity to hear the unfiltered truth from the ground floor, rather than versions of filtered truth that might have otherwise been provided through successive layers of management.

> *"The nut of communications cannot be a 'stuck microphone'—always on send." Jim Donihee*

Flying high-performance aircraft such as the CF-18 Hornet generally puts you in an environment where things happen extremely fast and efficient communications are essential. Although uncommon, it did happen on occasion where the transmit button for the aircraft radios would get stuck in the transmit position. When that happened, the radio frequency was effectively jammed, and all you could hear was the heavy breathing or mutterings of the culprit pilot who was more than likely unaware that his radio was malfunctioning. We would say he or she was "stuck on send" because they was constantly transmitting and unaware of others' efforts to communicate effectively. They was unwittingly blocking communication from happening.

In that instance, it was a technical malfunction that prevented any chance for effective communications. The analogy of being "stuck on send" applies equally to a CEO or any senior leader who is so busy preaching or telling, that he or she never takes time to listen to understand the other points of view necessary for effective communications to take place. Without the opportunity for open frank exchange in the communications process, the risk of operations going sideways will be very high.

> *"If your impression is that because you're CEO, you can make a career out of just telling people what to do, you'll be on a very quick path to failure." – Jim Donihee*

Communications—Its Impact

We often say that diversity is our strength. The truth is that that strength can only be harnessed through effective communications to capture the best ideas and to ensure that everyone understands and is on the same page to execute. We all come to the table with our own life experiences that created a set of filters through which we each experience our world. In order to achieve complex business goals, we need effective planning, clear accountabilities, and excellence in execution. Effective communication is the thread that weaves its way through each of these critical elements of goal achievement. Only through effective communications can we ensure that our respective filters are not creating a different meaning for each of us along the way—do we share the same perceptions of reality? It is important to understand that arriving at different meanings isn't intentional, it's simply the product of the filters and biases that we each carry with us. Therefore, the need is to ensure a free and open exchange of communication that confirms a shared understanding of the messages being exchanged.

"Communication works for those who work at it." – John Powell

The sum of these interactions and communications are effectively embedded in the results-based model we've seen previously:

- Reality—we arrived at a shared view of reality and where / how improvements would be achieved;

- Affinity—we increased affinity amongst team members through exposure, humility and authenticity; and

- Communications—effective communications provide the avenue through which true contact and understanding can be achieved.

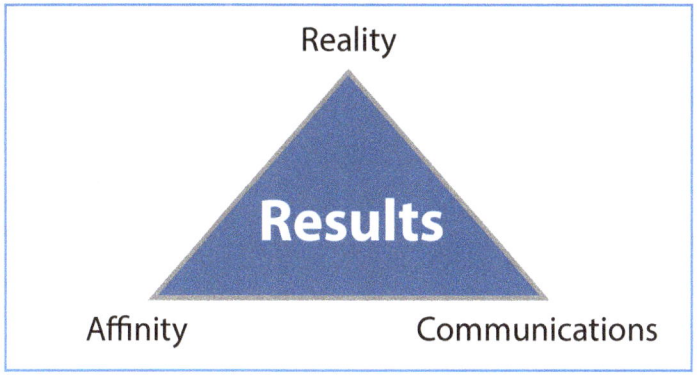

Figure 17 – The ARC Triangle

SUMMARY POINTS

✓ In communications, being authentic trumps trying to be profound.

✓ NLP provides a valuable model that illustrates the filters and unintended barriers to effective communications.

✓ Face-to-face communications are the most effective to win hearts and minds.

✓ Engaging your work force through an array of touchpoints will ensure they come to know you, and that you better understand the challenges they face.

✓ Don't be "stuck on send"—ensure you engage and listen with the aim of understanding.

✓ If diversity is to be a strength in your company, make sure you communicate effectively to make the most of it.

ACTION POINTS

✓ Strive to be authentic and genuine rather than profound in your communications.

✓ Engage people from across your workforce to assess how consistent your view of reality is—listen to understand rather than respond if their view of reality differs from your own.

✓ Examine your personal filters with the intention of determining whether they help or hinder your effectiveness.

14

PERSONAL GROWTH AND DEVELOPMENT

"We can't solve problems by using the
same kind of thinking we used when we created them."
– Albert Einstein

The journey that you will travel from the outset of starting your business to seeing it fully mature will impose incredible demands on you. Throughout that period, which could last many years, it'll be essential that you continuously invest in yourself, your personal growth and development, at least as much as you invest in your business. During those initial heady times you'll be called upon to do it all. Essentially, you'll be working deeply *'in the business.'* You will be deeply invested in every aspect of your business, which is understandable if you put all your personal equity in, or if you've had to make personal loan guarantees in order to gather the initial working capital. As you grow, however, you will need to evolve and constantly raise your capabilities and level of thinking to anticipate and stay ahead of the problems and challenges that will confront you. Your ability to evolve and grow to working *'on the business'* rather than working in the business will ultimately determine your success. Throughout the journey, self-awareness and ensuring you grow yourself will be critical. Far too many high-potential start-up businesses have stalled and ultimately failed because the entrepreneurial CEO wasn't able to grow and evolve at a pace that permitted the individual to lead the company.

"In a nutshell, hard experience has taught me that real leadership
is about understanding yourself first, then using that to create
a superb organization." – Capt. (N) M. Abrashoff

Moving from working in the business to working on the business will challenge you personally. Your ability to step back, to zoom out so to speak, and take a holistic snapshot of yourself and your business as if you were an objective observer will be key. Expanding your perspective at every level—personal, professional, and industry-wide—will have a huge impact on your ability to lead a rapidly growing organization. Investing in yourself so you have a firm grasp of your inner workings—your strengths, limitations, and how to improve upon them—is a quest you must be open to.

Self-Awareness—You can't do it all

One of the earliest leadership examples where self-awareness played a significant role in my life was in my third year of military college in Saint-Jean-sur-Richelieu, Quebec. I don't recall how it happened, but I found myself in charge of organizing and leading the annual Military Tattoo, which was a major event that showcased all of the military and athletic skills we were developing as students at the military college. The event involved some 350 participants to be showcased in front of an audience of more than 2000 attendees. I knew at this early stage of my own leadership development that I had some strong skills in a number of areas where I felt at ease and in flow when exercising them. However, I also knew there were several areas that were simply not my sweet spots, and that I would fail if I tried to control everything. That degree of self-awareness permitted me to build a team that complemented my strengths and filled in around my weaknesses. Lowering my own self-importance, recognizing the gaps in my own knowledge and capabilities, and focusing on the mission lead to a highly successful event.

Leading up to the event, and before planning and selecting the leadership team, I sat down and pondered over a very simple model that we had recently covered in our military leadership and behavioural psychology classes. The model, called the Johari Window model, provides a powerful but remarkably straightforward tool for understanding self-awareness in relation to the mission and goals you need to achieve. By examining the model in relation to myself, I was able to identify potential blind spots as well as unknowns that introduced significant risk to successfully leading and executing the Tattoo. I was then able to select and engage the leadership team that lead to a highly successful event.

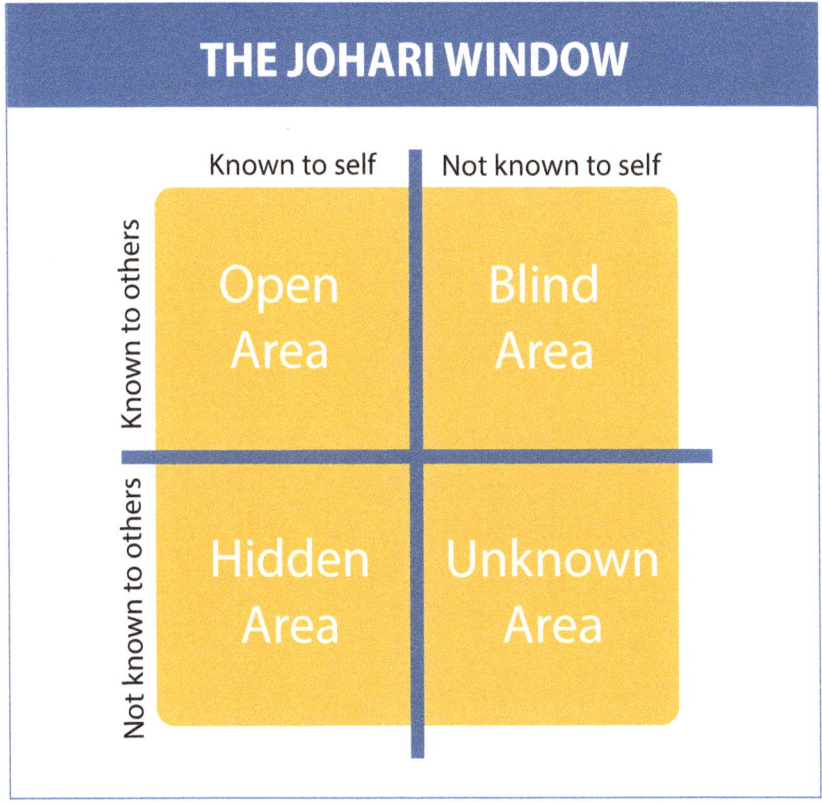

Figure 18 – The Johari Window

As a leader and CEO, the key questions that arise from looking at this simple model are:

1. How do I identify and reduce my personal blind spots as quickly and effectively as possible?

2. How do I shrink the unknown area to diminish business risks?

3. What boundaries do I want to set in relation to self-disclosure and exposure?

4. Who can I engage to provide candid feedback on my performance?

You'll find the answer to these questions through humility, curiosity, and continuous investment in yourself.

Another valuable tool related to circumspection is the personal Strength, Weakness, Opportunity and Threat analysis (SWOT). While most are likely familiar with its use as an analytical tool that's valuable to assess business strategies, it can also prove highly useful when examining personal abilities. In the same manner as the Johari Window, the personal SWOT can reveal key personal attributes, as well as personal soft spots that require attention. Devoting time and thought yourself and asking a few key stakeholders to provide feedback by completing the analysis through the lens of *carefrontation* that we've previously discussed can prove invaluable. While there are many templates widely available, the following example provides clear insight into the deliberateness and objectivity you need to assert as you complete the review. In your mind's eye, it's helpful to zoom out to a hundred thousand feet and observe yourself from the perspective of an objective evaluator. Typical questions might be:

- How do you relate?

- What sets you apart?

- What qualifies you?

- What are your greatest weaknesses / opportunities for improvement?

A sample personal SWOT template is set out below:

	POSITIVE	NEGATIVE
	Strengths	**Weaknesses**
Internal	What are your strengths relative to others	Where do you fall short of others
	What do you have access to that others do not	How do you fare on a skills / knowledge matrix
	What are your proudest accomplishments and how do they map up against this role / opportunity	What do you most dislike doing that this role / opportunity requires
	What do colleagues say are your strengths	What do colleagues see as your weaknesses
	Skills and Attributes might include: leadership, commercial skills, communications skills, strategy development, BD skills, Public / Capital markets access / knowledge, technical / engineering skills, proven experience in the field, people skills / personal awareness, beliefs and values that set you apart	Detractors might include: close minded, reactive vs responsive, stretched technically or in leadership capabilities, controlling, lacking humility, expecting rather than dedicated, weak financial discipline, untested leadership
	Opportunities **(Not in your control)**	**Threats** **(Not in your control)**
External	Market requirement / unfulfilled	What obstacles exist
	Significant complaints about a missing service offering	What problems could undermine your planning
	Capturing / applying an emerging technology	Which weaknesses could become threats
	Emergent economic trends / demands	Emergent economic or competitive trends / demands, time pressures
	Examples include: knowledge / networks to engage and build upon	Examples include: life changing events that undermine your availability or capabilities

Table 9 – Example of Personal SWOT

Investing in yourself can take many forms, whether by participating in industry associations, engaging a personal coach, or participating in one of the many CEO Mastermind groups that are available. I will declare my personal bias by stating that while you can garner a lot of valuable knowledge and networking from industry associations, they do not match the degree of personal accountability you anchor in on with a personal coach. Furthermore, if you choose one of the CEO Mastermind groups, you will frequently parallel the degree of personal accountability you get with a coach, while tremendously augmenting the wisdom and knowledge derived from CEO peers leading companies of various sizes and scope across different industries. When you participate fully in these groups, fully vested as each other's most caring critics and support each other's success, the value you obtain is far beyond the price tag for membership.

CEO Mastermind Group—Success Case in Point

While serving as the Chief Operating Officer for Canada's National Energy Board, I was tapped on the shoulder one day and asked by a friend, who was the CEO of an oilfield services company, if I would consider joining a CEO Mastermind group. They were looking to round out the peer group of CEOs by adding a senior executive leader from the public sector. The group was comprised of CEOs from several sectors including Oil & Gas, marketing, hospitality, housing construction, vehicle sales, biotechnology, aeronautics, venture capital, and others. The diversity of the industries brought a powerhouse of knowledge to the table, and the calibre of leaders set an example to step up to. The group met monthly for one full day, which was devoted to topics of business effectiveness and CEO well-being, while also providing a forum where business problems and challenges could be presented. This group of 'carefrontational' peers critiqued your strategies, tested your theories, and added to them to ensure success. The group's true value was the fact that the members cared deeply about each other and their respective success. They would speak the truth, hold each other to account, and never blow smoke at one another.

After several years as a member of this group, I was invited to take over as the chairperson when the previous leader retired. Soon after taking over the group, one of our members, who was the CEO of a new and still relatively small marketing firm, came to the group seeking advice regarding a significant business opportunity. His firm had been invited to bid on the marketing contract for a major motorsports' equipment manufacturer. Should he win the contract, it was clear that the profile, volume, and value of the work would launch his company into an entirely new league and level of play. Talented as this young CEO was, this was a level of bid that required an entirely new level of sophistication, confidence, and polish when presenting to the selection committee. His initial presentation to our CEO peer group was solid, but lacked the lustre required to leave a winning impression. The feedback was quite direct and left him anxious about preparing for the final bid presentations, which were to take place over the next several days.

After spending a couple of painstaking days reworking his bid and presentation based on the advice he had received, he again presented to a subset of our CEO group. The results were like night and day. Later that week, when he and his team submitted their bid and presented to the company's selection committee, he found out that his firm had been selected for a multiyear, multimillion-dollar contract. Needless to say, the value that he and his company received from participating in that CEO Mastermind group vastly exceeded the price tag. The major point here is that it would have been very easy to convince himself that the investment in the Mastermind group was too expensive at this age and stage of his company. By acknowledging his need for continuous growth and choosing a forum that held him accountable, he was able to accelerate his personal growth and the growth of this company while substantially reducing the risks it faced.

The lessons

"When we are no longer able to change a situation, we are challenged to change ourselves." – Viktor E. Frankl

Personal growth and self-awareness will be absolutely key to your success and that of your company's in the journey that lies ahead. In the example of this young CEO mapped up against the Johari window, we can see that his commitment to growth and self-awareness through his affiliation with the CEO Mastermind Group substantially reduced his blind spots, provided him access to cross-sectoral wisdom, and topped it off with a group of dedicated leaders who shared accountability and commitment to each other's success. He drew benefit from the experience and continues to be a CEO Mastermind member many years later.

In the end, the lesson is not so much that you need to be part of a CEO Mastermind group, but that you need a conscious and dedicated approach to your own personal growth.

Leading means growing your capabilities, knowledge, and quality of leadership. That means that throughout your journey you will need to master the ability to *zoom out* and *zoom in*. Zooming out means routinely taking a disciplined, holistic look at you and your company, at its strengths and weaknesses, and how it is positioned in the marketplace. It means questioning how your company is performing objectively and critically with you at the helm. Zooming in means taking a hard, objective look at yourself from a place of humility, having set aside your self-importance and ego to get a true perspective of where and how you need to grow to continue leading your company.

There is a monumental difference between simply occupying the position of CEO and leading.

SUMMARY POINTS

- ✓ Higher levels of thinking are required to evolve and succeed—that requires a dedicated growth and development strategy for you and your business.

- ✓ Your ability to grow and work on rather than in the business will determine your success.

- ✓ Expanding your self-awareness and lowering yourself-importance go hand-in-hand.

- ✓ Simple models such as the Johari Window can provide powerful insights to focus your growth and development.

- ✓ Surround yourself with people who care so deeply for you that they will tell you the truth.

- ✓ Even more importantly, create the conditions so they will tell you the truth.

ACTION POINTS

✓ Conduct a personal SWOT and contrast your personal skills and attributes against those that are critical for the next levels of success your business needs to achieve.

✓ Seek candid, direct, wide-ranging feedback regarding your strengths and weaknesses.

✓ Develop and execute a plan to close the gaps, either by hiring, or by learning and growing (coaching / mentoring).

15

CONSCIOUS LEADERS—AWAKENED LIVES

"Profitability is a shallow goal if it
doesn't have a real purpose."
– Howard Schultz, Starbucks CEO

Unless you continue to grow both personally and professionally, unless you continue to stretch and become more, you run the risk of becoming the choke point that stifles your business's success. Throughout this book, I've been guiding you to think about working *'on your business'* rather than *'in your business'* to make sure you are successful. Throughout the entire journey of building and growing your business, it is equally important to think about who is working on you.

Working on yourself to actively explore your limits and beliefs and working to consciously define your unique purpose so that it aligns with the business you're building will make the journey exceedingly more enjoyable. When your personal purpose is aligned with the journey you're undertaking, that journey will be far more enjoyable and feel a lot less like work. Knowing yourself and the depth of your potential will allow you to grow your capabilities, remain calm and open, and to be fully present in the midst of the storms and tremendous stresses you will undoubtedly face. When you can truly hold that space and be present during those challenging times, rather than reacting and becoming short or demanding when under pressure, you will become a source of confidence and inspiration for your workforce.

Knowing yourself so you can fully become a "Conscious Leader," rather than one who is shackled by limiting beliefs and unyielding habits, will ensure you are able to grow and remain worthy of leading the company you're building. The nature of people making up today's workforce is changing rapidly. Workers are no longer willing to settle in and take instructions the way many of us did when we commenced our careers. They are more aware, more conscious, and have much higher expectations of the companies and firms where they will devote their talents. To fully engage their time and skills, you will need to cultivate your comfort and presence in the face of sincere and direct questions that they will put to you. In short, you will need to look deep inside yourself to be clear about who you are so you can engage their hearts and minds because a power-based command and control style of leadership will not land well with them.

The changing expectations of these young professionals you will need to engage are highly reflective of society's changing expectations overall. In the recent past, indicators such as the Edelman Trust Barometer clearly highlight the expectations that businesses must play a more meaningful role in solving significant social and environmental issues. Institutional investors are increasingly moving towards companies that rate highly across metrics pertaining to the environment, sustainability, and governance (ESG) index. Sometimes nicknamed Firms of Endearment (FoEs), these types of companies have embraced social capitalism and are striving to work more cooperatively with customers, suppliers, employees, and the communities in which they reside and operate. Some of the findings that characterize these companies are set out in the table that follows.

THE FIRMS OF ENDEARMENT—OPERATING CHARACTERISTICS :
• Their vision and purpose go beyond making money.
• They strive to align themselves with the interests of all stakeholders.
• Executive salaries are modest in relation to competitors.
• They have a strong, pervasive open-door policy based on integrity and transparency.
• Employee compensation and benefits exceed those of their competitors.
• They out-distance competitors in employee training and empowerment.
• Their employee turnover and marketing costs are considerably lower than the industry average.
• They make a conscious effort to hire people who are passionate about the company and its products.
• They honour the spirit of the law and not just a letter of the law.
• They consider their culture to be their greatest asset and primary source of competitive advantage. Typical characteristics inherent in their cultures are: ◦ Trust   ◦ Loyalty and respect   ◦ Belonging and oneness   ◦ Caring and fun

In many ways, Firms of Endearment have recognized and positioned themselves for the unfolding changes in our societies. There is a societal shift occurring, which some have now labelled "The Age of Transcendence," a time when we are moving from the rational, materialistic perspectives associated with the left brain to the more emotional and intuitive perspectives associated with the right brain. As these changes become more deeply rooted, it will become even more important to work on you so that you remain well-positioned to lead and grow your company accordingly. The graphic which follows illustrates the flow and impact that you, as CEO, will induce on your organization. Your worldview, awareness, and capabilities will impact your organization. Working on you will strengthen your advantage.

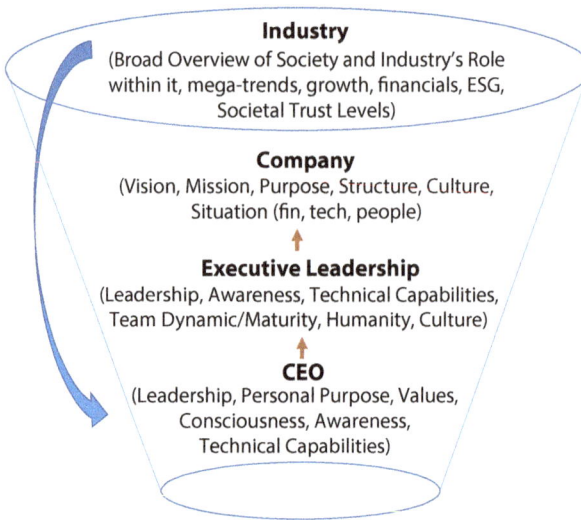

Figure 19 – CEO Impact

As depicted above, the worldview you develop needs to be considered in order to drive your own personal development including your leadership, self-awareness, and technical capabilities. Developing emotional intelligence is valuable, but developing self-awareness, especially in terms of your limiting beliefs and underlying habitual patterns, will dramatically improve your resilience, presence, and leadership capabilities. The strengths that you possess and the person that you are will have a dramatic impact on your executive leadership team and, through them, on the company as a whole. Engaging mentors, advisors, and coaches to assist you in exploring and improving your attitudes, beliefs, and depth of self-awareness will ensure you don't become self-limiting.

> *"If you treat your employees like they make a difference, they will." – Dr. Jim Goodnight*

Your ability to generate success couldn't be any more succinctly expressed than in the statement cited above. Almost unwittingly this is the key principle that I've lived by and been led by throughout my career. At the time, I didn't recognize the patterns I was following. As I look back now, however, I can see the connection between these dots and more deeply understand the strong results that we achieved.

The 410 Squadron Experience

When I was first assigned to 410 Operational Training Squadron as its Commanding Officer, I was discouraged. The squadron, which is tasked with training Canada's CF-18 pilots, was not renowned amongst our fighter force as the place to be. While it was a workhorse and did incredibly good work, it didn't benefit from operational deployments and the training mandate didn't provide any flexibility in how it conducted its operations. In short, people worked too hard, they didn't seem to matter, and the pilots' training was in need of an overhaul. I was blessed to have an exceptional Chief Warrant Officer (Chief Superintendent) and, together, working as conscious leaders, we set about turning the place around.

In the months that followed, we reinvigorated the vision and mission of the organization, which was comprised of about 350 personnel. We stressed the interconnectedness of everyone in the organization and worked hard to reinstall pride into the work completed by the squadron. We effectively went from a transactional leadership style to a transformational leadership model that raised the organization's level of consciousness. We reinstituted squadron deployments where the squadron members worked hard, truly got to know and depend on one another, and we also managed some impressive fun. Along the way, we elevated and empowered every one of the squadron members by learning their names and backgrounds, and by making sure they each knew, on a personal level, how much they mattered.

Over the course of two years, we completely transformed the course materials used for instruction, achieved significant efficiencies in the flight hours required to train pilots, and developed the cohesiveness and esprit that made 410 Squadron the go-to squadron on the base. The Chief and I made it all about the people. As our personal standards were higher and we worked harder, the culture of the squadron became stronger and delivered much greater output. The language of pride and accountability was evident, as was the top to bottom alignment around our collective mission of "Training the Best Fighter Pilots in the World." I had grown both personally and professionally and, despite my initial discouragement on being assigned to 410 squadron, the turnaround we achieved by making it all about the people was one of the richest and most enjoyable experiences of my military career.

The deepest secret is to learn and authentically act upon the fact that when Leading, it is actually you who most needs to serve those you are privileged to lead. Serve them by creating clarity of mission, clarity of accountabilities, and by creating the environment and culture within which they can succeed.

> *If you truly want to be a leader…. "you must care fundamentally and deeply about people. If you can't find your way to that place, you'll never be anything other than a manager." – Jim Donihee*

The National Energy Board Experience

When I joined Canada's national energy regulator, the National Energy Board (NEB), as its Chief Operating Officer in 2004, I didn't have a solid picture of what I was stepping into. The personnel of the board, some 300 strong, had truly been overworked for several years. The organization had a heavy-handed top-down approach to leadership that didn't develop or look after its people. As a result, organizational consciousness was low, and it was bleeding professionals to an industry in hot pursuit of talent. Over the next three years, acting on many of the principles now reflected in Firms of Endearment and by developing conscious leadership, we turned the NEB around and saw it become recognized as a top 100 employer in Canada. We achieved that result because we made it all about the people.

Some of the measures that were put in place are described earlier chapters, but the key transformational changes were:

- Vision, Mission, and Values: We revisited the organization's vision, mission, and values we committed to live by. Everyone in the organization understood the expectations, especially that they applied even more stringently to senior leaders. Everyone understood that accountability and compassion applied to all.

- Increased Transparency and Accountability for Leaders: We introduced leadership development across the organization, strengthened performance management, and, most importantly, posted the performance contracts for all executive leaders on the internal website. This led to increased fairness, consistency, and openness to innovation and improvements.

- Appreciative Inquiry: We undertook a significant effort around appreciative inquiry. We challenged the entire organization to look for the good in what we were doing and, more importantly, in the people who were doing it. We did not look through rose-coloured glasses, nor did we blow smoke at one another, but we did embed trust and respect while eliminating a great deal of bureaucracy. The language of appreciation overwrote the language of negativity and criticism and uplifted the entire organization.

- Compensation and benefits: We went to bat for the personnel working at the NEB and succeeded in winning some significant gains in compensation and benefits. While we still significantly lagged industry in terms of compensation, the balance of all the changes we instituted largely stemmed the tide of attrition. In the end, the increased fairness and transparency for everyone in the organization resulted in the union's accepting pay for performance. This, in turn, diminished expectations founded on seniority and entitlement and replaced them with understanding and a desire to contribute.

Looking back, I can now see the pattern in these two instances in which I was involved. Quite simply, it was all about the people. Raising the collective level of consciousness by invoking clear and impactful people-based leadership led to amazing results. While there was obviously a great deal of work involved over a considerable time, it was simply about the people. Making sure that they knew they mattered, they had a voice, and that I cared deeply about them. I was more than willing to demonstrate my vulnerability because I didn't have all the answers. And, most importantly, they knew I had their backs; they knew I expected the highest standards of performance; they knew I would be firm and fair, and that we'd have some pretty healthy fun along the way.

> *"Your Organization Can't be any more conscious or*
> *aware than You, so work on You." – Jim Donihee*

The lesson that's incredibly important to draw from all this is that your organization, the company that you're building, cannot be any more conscious or aware than you! Your presence, comfort levels, self-awareness, beliefs, and limiting beliefs will define you as a person, especially as a leader. Your ability to create a strong invitation and elicit the absolute best from your people will absolutely define the quality of dialogue that takes place at your executive table and throughout your company. What you tolerate in yourself or at your executive table will become prevalent throughout the organization. If you lean in and come from an imposing, ego-based style of leadership, you will shut down the best and brightest and end up being surrounded by teams of minions. So, as your company grows and complexity increases, and as you grow from working in the business to working on the business in order to stay ahead, it is even more vital that you work on you. Work on you so that you can increase your awareness and consciousness of who you are: address your competencies, your triggers and limitations, and your inner critic and limiting beliefs.

> *"Throughout my career and my life, there has been one essential truth: the biggest opportunity for improvement—in business, at home, and in life—is awareness." – Alan Mulally*

Greater self-knowledge will lead to greater confidence and authenticity, which will be invaluable to you as a CEO. You have to reach inside yourself to find your truth because you can't resonate with the people you're leading without it. If you're pretending and have simply tried to somehow strap on the identity of a leader your people will know in a heartbeat. You have to be able to speak from your heart, authentically, and do it in a way that speaks to other people's hearts. Deliberately working at raising your own consciousness and ability to create deep connections and safe spaces for the most difficult conversations will lay down the cornerstones of success. A recent article in *Forbes* magazine laid out the premise beautifully when it stated "it shouldn't be a stretch to understand that the internal dynamics at play inside every human at a company and particularly in its CEO and leadership team, inform the quality of consciousness of the company itself."

The graphic that follows illustrates the realities that we experience as leaders, the external symptoms, which are reflective of the internal dialogue. In your case as CEO, the internal dialogue represents the kind of work that you need to do in order to be fully present as a leader. When you are not able to resolve the dialogue yourself, you can expect the challenges to ripple across your executive team and throughout your organization.

THE LIFE / ORGANIZATION YOU'VE CREATED

What you get on the outside, is driven by
what's going on in the inside.

The External Symptom	The Internal Dialogue
Hesitation / Inaction / Missing Targets	Lack of Clarity ~ Vision, Intentions &
Exhaustion / Health Issues	Accountabilities / Avoidance
Unacceptable Behaviours / Guilt / Biases	Clarity of Priorities, Training & Delegation
Superficial Relationships	Values & Beliefs, Blind Spots
Disharmony & People Challenges	Guarded & Closed / Lacking Authenticity
Feeling Trapped	Lack of Contact, Accountability & Expectations
Sleepless Nights	False Nobility / Lack of Boundaries
Isolation	Mind Chatter & Anxiety
	Lack of Presence & Vulnerability

Figure 20 – Outside is Driven by the Inside

Impact: How are you choosing to grow?

CEOs are typically voracious readers. Undoubtedly reading can stimulate some deep reflection but it rarely generates the depth of engagement that is needed to effect lasting change and measurable growth. To become the exceptional leader that you aspire to be, and your company merits, you will have to grow professionally in terms of knowledge and skills related to the business, and, equally importantly, you will have to grow personally. Confucius believed that learning and growth come through one of three forms: 1) reflection, which is the noblest; 2) imitation via coaching or mentorship, which is the easiest and fastest; and 3) experience, which is often the bitterest and slowest. Which of these three are you choosing and how's that working for you?

There's an entirely new wave of employees entering the workforce; they are characterized by different expectations and for a purpose higher than simply generating profits. For that reason, the level of consciousness that you attain and your ability to engage their hearts and minds will determine whether you can attract and retain the most talented and committed individuals going forward. Firms of Endearment are demonstrating that stronger commitments to the environment, sustainability, and governance set the course to stronger returns. To ensure you can grow and position your company to succeed you'll need to move from working in the business to working on the business all the while—and perhaps most importantly—working on you.

SUMMARY POINTS

✓ You will need to grow from working in the business to working on the business, all the while working on you.

✓ The level of consciousness, self-awareness, and presence you cultivate in yourself will dictate how your executive team operates and that will ripple throughout the organization.

✓ Workers of today, and certainly those of tomorrow, expect companies to achieve a higher purpose than simply making profits.

✓ Institutional investors are already moving towards companies that rate highly in ESG metrics.

✓ Firms of Endearment are breaking away from the pack and outperforming "good to great" companies.

✓ It is all about the people—provided you're capable of engaging their hearts and minds.

✓ Your level of consciousness, your internal dialogue, and how effectively you grow and resolve it will determine how you and your company succeed.

ACTION POINTS

✓ Identify your own life purpose and contrast it to that of your business to strengthen alignment.

✓ Assess your company against the operating characteristics of FoEs.

✓ Seek feedback, identify your personal "external symptoms," and do the internal work to address them.

✓ Surround yourself with trusted advisors, mentors, and coaches to challenge you and to increase your level of consciousness.

✓ Develop a learning and growth strategy for yourself, both personally and professionally, and act on it.

16

CONTINUED IMPACT: IN YOUR SERVICE

Since retiring (again) from the corporate sector, I've created HighFlight Executive Consulting in order to continue serving and creating impact. I've been blessed to coach CEOs and aspiring executives, as well as serving on advisory, corporate, and not-for-profit boards working to create greater personal and corporate performance. Working with people from around our continent and internationally, I particularly enjoy coaching and growing their capacity to generate impact from a place of greater confidence, founded on awareness and authenticity. This life isn't a practice life—we were meant to enjoy the journey while living, leading, and achieving with ease.

My Passion: Provide the coaching and mentorship you will benefit from

The journey you're traveling will be one of continuously striving to find balance between your goals and aspirations, and rest and rejuvenation to ensure you get there in one piece. If you focus only on the goals and aspirations, you will 'consume' yourself and be unable to operate at peak performance. I've lived it and far too often observed when CEOs become so consumed with the chase, that everything else around them is ignored and suffers accordingly. Health suffers, relationships suffer, and you become reactive and lose perspective. Always remember, this is not a practice life; this is your life.

The life that you create will result from the sum of all the choices that you make along the way – you are the creator, not the victim. Those choices will be underpinned by your awareness and self-knowledge [or lack thereof], and your ability to challenge yourself to define the reality you want while acknowledging and working to close the gap between that and the reality you're currently living. Self-care throughout your journey will ensure you equip yourself to go the distance. Self-care includes the personal development you'll require as well as the health and wellness investments you'll make to enjoy your life. Deferring family time, health and personal development and the enjoyment of life to some future date is a mistake I observe all too often. Thinking you'll be ready to throw the switch and suddenly become happy at some future date because of the things you've achieved and the money you've made is a sure way to lose sight of what's meaningful. Yes, there will certainly be times when you must sprint, but if you're entire life is consumed and lived as a sprint you will achieve a perpetual state of stress and dis-ease that will almost assuredly become one of disease. Happiness and fulfilment are not things that are 'out there' somewhere. They come from within and only you can unlock that door.

Developing and sustaining an awareness of the life you're creating will be invaluable in the process of choice over reaction. By working with a partner in developing your success, one who can assist you in choosing wisely along the way will ensure you keep the 5 Fs [finance, family, fitness, fun and faith/spirituality] in perspective as you create a life of success and fulfilment.

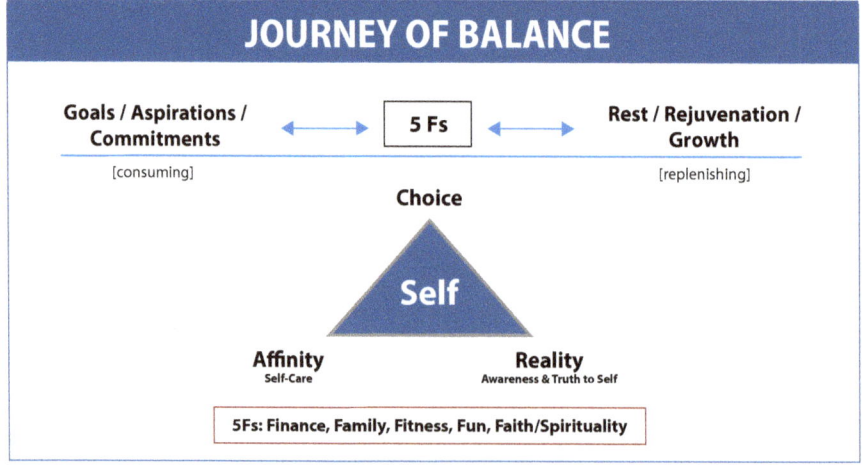

Figure 21 – Effective Balance

As you will have read throughout the book I have always been, and remain, passionate about leadership, people, and organizational excellence. Throughout my journey, I have been blessed with diverse leadership roles that afforded me tremendous opportunities to grow personally and professionally. Passing those lessons along, so as to accelerate the growth and development of today's leaders, is now my mission. By serving as a highly trusted accountability partner, I can ensure your leadership journey is accelerated by passing on my deep expertise in leadership, organizational effectiveness, strategy, and operational excellence in ways that continue to serve and create the impact you're looking for.

I know the loneliness, anxiety, and stress that CEOs and executives often experience, and I know it doesn't have to be that way. By acting with greater clarity and confidence in your leadership, you will regain balance and enjoy success across all areas of your life.

Working with me you will:

- Gain a trusted confidante who listens and is dedicated to ensuring you excel;
- Get clarity on who you are, what you want to achieve, and where you need to grow;
- Accelerate your growth and focus your leadership;
- Clarify your strategy, create a clear plan of attack, and act on it;
- Align and galvanize your teams toward organizational excellence;
- Broaden your perspective, eliminate stress, and succeed in life with greater ease.

I work with:

- Leaders who are committed to growth and want to make an impact;
- Leaders who invest in themselves as a precursor to success.

The way I work:

- One-on-one with CEOs and executive leaders—remotely and in person;
- Contracted high-impact engagements to identify, prioritize, and accelerate progress;

- Purpose specific engagements focused on trust, CEO and Executive Team effectiveness, culture, and leadership development.

Reach out:

Connect with me to find out how my knowledge, experience, and services will accelerate your growth and success. My aim is to ensure that you excel.

Jim Donihee, OMM CD
Colonel (Ret'd)
Email: jim@highflightexec.com or jimdonihee@gmail.com
Phone: 403-608-9003 in Calgary.

MY VISION:	MY MISSION:
Leadership Unleashed	To Ensure You Excel

WORKS CITED

Abrashoff, Michael. 2002. It's Your Ship - Management Techniques from the Best Damn Ship in the Navy. New York: Warner Business Books.

Angelou, Maya. 2020. GoodReads. July. Accessed July 2020. https://www.goodreads.com/quotes.

Archilochus. 2020. Work Management Insights. Accessed July 2020. https://www.workmanagementinsights.com.

Aristotle. n.d.

Ashkenas, Ron. 2002. The Boundaryless Organization. San Fransisco: Jossey-Bass.

Baker, Carlos. n.d. Ernest Hemingway Selected Letters 1917-1961.

Collins, Jim. 2001. Good To Great. Random House Business Books.

Covey, S. n.d.

Creech, Bill. 1994. The Five Pillars of TQM: How to Make Total Quality Management Work for You. New York: Truman Talley Books.

Daniels, Aubrey. 2019. Aubrey Daniels International. https://www.aubreydaniels.com.

Davis, J. Straw M. Scullard S. Kikkonen B. 2013. The Work of Leaders. Wiley.

Einstein, Albert. 2012. Insider. 19 April. Accessed 2020. https://www.businessinsider.com/we-cant-solve-problems.

Evans, Henry. 2008. Winning With Accountability: The Secret Language of High Performing Organizations. Dallas: CornerStone Leadership Institute.

Ford, Henry. n.d.

Frankl, Victor. 2014. Man's Search for Meaning. Boston: Beacon Press.

Goodnight, Jim. 2017. Forbes. 27 September. Accessed July 2020. https://www. forbes.com/sites/gilpress/2017/09/27.

Heller, Robert. 2001. Jack Welch. New York: Dorling Kindersley Limited.

Jobs, Steve. n.d.

Kawasaki, Guy. 2011. Enchantment - The Art of Changing Hearts,Minds and Actions. London: Penguin Group.

Lencioni, Patrick. 2005. Overcoming The Five Dysfunctions of Teams. San Francisco: Jossey-Bass.

—. 2002. The Five Dysfunctions of Teams. San Francisco: Jossey-Bass.

Lobovitz, G. 1997. The Power of Alignment. New York: John Wiley & Sons, Inc.

Luccock, H.E. 1961.

Maister, David. n.d. The Trusted Advisor.

Miller, Mark. 2011. The Secret of Teams. San Francisco: Berrett-Koehler.

Morgan, Gwyn. 2003. EnCana Corporate Constitution.

Mulally, Alan. 2017. 99u. 17 August. Accessed August 2020. https://99u.adobe. com/articles/56000/hot-to-become-more-self-aware.

Myers, Harry. 1932. Human Engineering. New York: Harper & Brothers.

Powell, John. n.d. AZ Quotes. https://www.azquotes/quote/536785.

Proctor, Bob. n.d. Bob Proctor Quotes. https://quotefancy.com/ bob-proctor-quotes.

Schultz, Howard. 2013. Huffpost. 28 June. Accessed July 2020. https://www. huffpost.com/entry/starbucks-profitability.

Simos, Paul. 2019. Paul Simos. 3 May. Accessed July 2020. https://paulsimos. medium.com.

Sisodia, Raj. 2014. Firms of Endearment. New Jersey: Pearson Education.

Sisodia, Raj Wolfe, David Sheth, Jag. 2014. Firms of Endearment. New Jersey: Pearson Education.

Toffler, Alvin. n.d.

Tzu, Sun. 1983. The Art of War. New York: Bantam Doubleday Dell Publishing Group Inc.

Welch, Jack. 2001. Straight From The Gut. New York: Warner Books.

Whitaker, Steve Gruenert & Todd. 2015. School Culture Rewired: How to Define, Assess, and Transform It. Alexandria.

"Expect your copy of this book to be well dog-eared and beautifully used up in 10 years as you will want to revisit its pages many times. Jim Donihee's Leadership journey from single-seat fighter pilot, military leader to the private sector C-suite draws a beautiful contrast that will inspire in you a different context for leadership. From powerful skills and mindsets leaders must embody to the limitations we must shed, this book will inspire a new level of leadership in today's rapid change, high stress world."

TERESA DE GROSBOIS

#1 INTERNATIONAL BESTSELLING AUTHOR OF *MASS INFLUENCE*,

FOUNDER AND CHAIR EVOLUTIONARY BUSINESS COUNCIL

"Every once and in a while, a book comes across your desk that captures a level of authenticity, practicality and heart that most simply cannot. This, my friends, is one of those books. Having seen Jim work in many different theatres of leadership, this compilation of his military and civilian experiences is a clear road map for new and seasoned leaders alike. If you're new to the game or looking to reinvigorate the people around you, Jim's real-life purpose-driven approach is something you can put into practice immediately.

TYLER CHISHOLM

CEO, CLEARMOTIVE MARKETING

PODCAST HOST – COLLISIONS YYC & THEY JUST GET IT

ABOUT THE AUTHOR

Colonel Jim M. Donihee, OMM, CD is a graduate of the Royal Military College in Saint-Jean, P.Q., and was a single-seat fighter pilot and senior military commander in both NORAD and NATO theatres of operations. Retiring a Decorated Leader after 28 years of military service, his subsequent career spanned senior executive leadership positions in industry, government and not-for-profit, all focused on creating and sustaining organizational excellence. He is the founder and CEO of HighFlight Executive Consulting and now passionately focuses on working with CEOs, Executive Teams, and high-potential leaders to unleash their Leadership to accelerate their journey to lives and businesses that exceed their dreams. You can visit his website at www.highflightexec.com.

"Hailing from decades of Leadership where life and death are moment to moment decisions, Jim has distilled the essence of what it takes to be a World Class Leader who is here to serve the biggest reach and impact. He has created here for you one of the most comprehensive tools to awaken your deepest authentic power with heart.

Jim's wisdom goes straight to the core and will leave you expanded, dialed in and ready to expand your most potent visions. The maturity and depth of his guidance has helped me attain new levels of consciousness, clarity, and resolve. Be ready to unleash the Warrior and wisdom within that will propel you beyond any and all limitations."

SATYEN RAJA

CEO WARRIORSAGE TRAININGS

"This is *the* essential manual for entrepreneurial leaders. Jim reveals the perspectives, skills and techniques, proven in battle and commerce, used by superior leaders to create resilient, formidable and competitive organizations. Designed as a an imminently readable reference, it contains specific elements and tools that are anchored by real world examples serving as a memory aid reinforcing the principles and demonstrating their real-world effectiveness.

Superior leadership is a lifelong journey and this manual will be the reader's touchstone. Take Jim's advice to heart and be prepared to be thrust to an unprecedented level of organizational and personal achievement."

TERRANCE KUTRYK

INDEPENDENT DIRECTOR AND PAST CEO ALLIANCE PIPELINE